Your Old English Sheepdog

By Alice J. Boyer

Compiled and Edited by
William W. Denlinger and R. Annabel Rathman

Cover design by
Bruce Parker

DENLINGER'S PUBLISHERS, LTD.
Box 76, Fairfax, Virginia 22030

Dedication

To ANNE WEISSE and to her "Fuzzy Butts," past and present:

SHAGGY BOY	CISSIE
SUSIE	THUMPER
SMUDGE	TOVI
JUNIOR	EMMY
BAMBI	TILLY
NONNIE	JENNY

and the cat, TAR BABY

Copyright© 1978

By William W. Denlinger, Fairfax, Virginia 22030. All rights reserved, including the right to reproduce this book, or portions thereof, in any form, except for the inclusion of brief quotations in a review. This book was completely manufactured in the United States of America.

International Standard Book Number: 0-87714-048-0

Library of Congress Catalog Card Number: 75-41985

The Author, Alice J. Boyer, and "Penny."

Foreword

I make no apology to feminists for using "he," "him," and "his" in referring to the Old English Sheepdog in this book. The masculine should, of course, be taken (where not inappropriate) to include the feminine. Perhaps I could have written about "she," "her," and "hers," but old habits are strong ones, and anyway, the women's lib movement came too late for my generation to serve in the front lines.

Be that as it may, one can't imagine referring to any Sheepdog as "it." There simply isn't an appropriate neuter word in any language I know that can be associated with a personality like the Sheepdog.

Through Sheepdogs I have come to admire and respect all dogs, and I am fond of all breeds—a few, I confess, perhaps a little more than others. Our youngsters selected the Old English Sheepdog to be our family dog ten years ago, and I have never from the moment of meeting our first puppy regretted the choice. A lot of fun, rewarding work, new activities, and many new friends have come our way in the years since, not to mention a number of additions to the census of Sheepdogs underfoot in the kitchen and now on the floor near me as I write this.

I have not been "in Sheepdogs" nearly so many years as any number of others, and I do not consider myself to be any sort of qualified expert. If, by writing the material for this book, I am able to help others who are perhaps just beginning in the breed, it is only because I have benefited for so long from the advice and encouragement of so many of those who have been devoted to the welfare and improvement of the breed longer than I have. I wish I could acknowledge my debt to each and every one of them here, but they are too many. I am sure they will understand and accept this general thanks in the interest of Sheepdogs everywhere.

I must, however, acknowledge with thanks my debt to the Old English Sheepdog Club of America, Inc., for permission to reprint the Breed Standard and to use records and statistics from their yearbooks and from their monthly publication, the *Old English Times* (formerly the *OESCA Bulletin*), and especially to Mrs. Karen Lee of Portland, Oregon, and to Mrs. Merle Downing of Newport, Virginia, who have so carefully and with so much dedication and effort collected and reported statistics for the club.

I also want to express my gratitude to the owners who so generously provided pictures of their dogs for this record; to Claudia Rodosky and Margareth Anne Boyer for the drawings reproduced here; and to Mr. John Mandeville of Montvale, New Jersey, and Mr. Lawrence Jones, of Champaign, Illinois, for their research in the area of breed history.

A. J. B.

Contents

Selecting the Puppy 7

The Adult Old English Sheepdog 15
   The Standard for the Old English Sheepdog 17
   Grooming the Old English Sheepdog for Show 25

Grooming the Family Dog 33

"Bed and Board" for the Family Dog 37

Maintaining the Dog's Health 43

History of the Genus *Canis* 57

Early History of the Old English Sheepdog 65

The Old English Sheepdog in the United States 73

Pillars of the Breed 83

Recent American Old English Sheepdogs of Note 91

The Old English Sheepdog as a Working Dog 115

The Personality of the Old English Sheepdog 123

Manners for the Family Dog 129

Show Competition 137
   Bench Shows 138
   Obedience Competition 143

Genetics 149

Breeding and Whelping 155

Reproduced on the front cover of this book is a picture of four Old English Sheepdogs with an authentic London Taxi that has almost become a trademark for Loyalblu Kennels. On the back cover is a picture of Ch. Farleydene Bartholomew, a sire of such agreeable temperament that he helped "mother" the puppies. Here a son, Fezziwig Ceiling Zero (five weeks), beards his father, cutting out a litter mate.

Peggotty Kennels' Ch. Camelot Sand 'n Pebbles with her puppies by Amr/Can/Bdn Ch. Fezziwig Vice Versa. Breeders-Owners, Charles and Janet Higley.

Loyalblu puppies ready for an outing. Breeders-Owners, Hugh and Linda Jordan.

"Chris" Shaw and his live Teddy Bears. Wagsend Kennels, Russell and Jane Shaw.

Selecting the Puppy

Whatever other puppies may be, Sheepdog puppies are more so. Utterly delightful in the litter, totally captivating and cuddlesome as individuals, their appeal is universal. No matter how many you may have, each is an individual in appearance, personality, and behavior, and any one of them is a perpetual source of entertainment, devotion, and companionship. Though fast growing (in some cases as much as ten pounds per month until about six months of age), they retain their clownish, bumblesome puppy behavior even after they are full grown.

What is a *good* Sheepdog like? He may be like the first one you ever knew. More likely, he will be like the first one you own. You may eventually confess, if only to yourself, that in a certain few respects he might possibly have been improved upon a little; but still, no matter if you end up with a number of them (as many have), you will forever carry in your memory the picture of your first Sheepdog as a good Sheepdog. How important it will be, then, to take the time to select your first one carefully.

Whether your purpose is to find a family pet or a dog for showing and breeding, there should be little difference in the selection process if you want a good, healthy, typical Sheepdog.

The buyer should get his puppy from someone who can give him information about the breed and the special care it requires, and who can advise him in his choice of the puppy that will best suit his particular needs. The only such person is a reputable breeder.

A reputable breeder can be found by inquiry among breed owners and handlers, especially at dog shows, and also through advertisements in the dog magazines. Probably one of the best indications of the breeder's merits is the care he takes to select his buyers to be sure that they intend to give the puppy a good home and that they are aware of the special needs of the breed and are able and willing to provide for them.

At a breeder's kennel you can see the puppy's dam and perhaps his sire, whose quality and temperament would be a clue to the potential of those qualities in the puppy. Then you can watch the puppy's behavior among his litter mates and the reaction of all of them to human beings. Here you may identify the quiet and shy puppy, the aggressive and lively one, the loner, and the sociable one. Puppies that have from the earliest days had plenty of human contact (loving and play) usually make better companions.

It is not always essential to see the breeder personally, however. Many good breeders can be relied upon to select one of their puppies for the buyer and ship it to him by air if they know his specific requirements.

The selection of the puppy should be based on two *equally* important factors: first, its individual characteristics of personality and temperament to suit the buyer's particular purposes, and second, its quality as a breed specimen (conformity to the Breed Standard). The latter judgment will require considerable study on the part of the newcomer to the breed before he will know what to look for.

Generally, the buyer who looks forward to enjoying quiet, restful evenings with a calm, gentle companion beside his chair should avoid selecting the over-exuberant, aggressive puppy who does not respond readily to human handling. The puppy destined for the show ring and breeding should not be the shy, nervous, loner of the litter. Each type has its place, but in the main, the basic nature of the puppy will not be changed much by training.

Select the strong, healthy puppy—the one that is lively, friendly, bright-eyed, clean, free of any abnormal discharge from eyes or ears, without skin lesions, and free of parasites, internal as well as external.

Selecting a puppy for conformation is a skill that requires a great deal of experience, and still the eventual outcome will be uncertain; time is the only proving factor. One should look for bone size and structure (including angulation); overall proportions that make for balance; firm muscle mass (the more of this, the better); and characteristics of movement, including a certain spirit or animation that may be summed up as "style."

Before he looks for a puppy, the buyer should learn about Hip Dysplasia. He should never hesitate to ask the breeder what he is doing to prevent its development in his puppies. Buy only from a breeder who x-rays his stock and breeds only to x-rayed stud dogs.

Avoid the puppy that tires quickly and so spends much time sitting (more often on one hip rather than squarely) when his litter mates are playing and moving about energetically. Avoid the excessively heavy puppy lest its early overweight bear too heavily on its developing hips; and the very thin puppy may also be a poor risk if the muscle mass is small and weak.

Regard with suspicion any breeder who pushes what he calls "perfectly-marked" puppies. While many people look for certain marking patterns (all-white heads, for example), this is purely a matter of personal preference, and the Standard allows for any pattern. Some exhibitors claim that many judges are reluctant to place a dog with a "splash"—that is, any prominent area of white in the midst of the darker coat on the dog's back or sides. In England recently there has been a movement advocating the adoption of a change in the Breed Standard to discourage this marking. Technically, it is not a fault at present under either the British or American Standard, but few fanciers want a dog with a splash for showing, despite the fact that there are champions that have it.

Eye color is largely a matter of preference, too, for the dog may have either brown or blue eyes (the darker, the better, in either case), or even one of each (this is the "wall-eyed" dog). While the Standard permits "a pearl, walleye or china eye" (in the singular), the large majority of fanciers agree that both eyes may acceptably be blue. The Standard does call a "light eye . . . most objectionable," however, which is understood to refer to lightness of tone in the brown eye only.

At eight weeks the black nose preferably should have no remaining spots of pink. Normally such spots will soon disappear, but not always.

While deafness is by no means a common occurrence in the breed, one should try to check for it in the puppy. The puppy should also be examined by a veterinary ophthalmologist for symptoms of congenital eye defects. Such problems have not so far been a special concern in the breed, but cautious breeders and buyers have recently begun to have such examinations made.

The key to success in living happily with a Sheepdog (or with any dog, as a matter of fact) is foresighted planning. It is better to avoid introducing a new puppy into the family at a time of preoccupation with holiday or personal festivities when ordinary home routine is not being followed.

For the first few days it would be advisable to keep the home atmosphere as nearly normal as possible, with a minimum of excitement and showing off the new puppy to friends. He requires time to adjust to his new situation, and you will have to be sure that he is given plenty of rest, which may be overlooked when

there are children eager to play with him or when vacation trips with him are undertaken immediately.

Transporting your puppy from the breeder to your home may involve merely an automobile trip with you. If so, you will want to stop with some frequency on a long trip to provide him with water and a little exercise. It is probably better to avoid feeding him during the trip if possible. A major concern will be to make sure that he does not become overheated in hot weather. NEVER leave him in a closed car, even in the shade; in fact, it would be better never to leave him alone in the car at all.

If the puppy is coming to you by air, the shipper should give you the flight number and arrival time in advance so that you can meet him. Try to avoid arranging an air shipment that will involve changing planes en route. On arrival he may be frightened. Any rough or exuberant play and general excitement can be postponed. Offer him water and a little quiet exercise before loading him into your car.

Have a supply of the puppy's customary food on hand for his arrival home. He can be changed gradually to any other food you prefer, but a sudden, complete changeover is likely to cause digestive problems, even with a full-grown dog. Follow your veter-

Puppies, four and a half weeks old, by Ch. Loyalblu Fascinatin Rhythm x Amy's Daisy Bell Diamond. Owners, Roger and Nancy Smith, Pinafore OES.

inarian's advice on feeding. Avoid overfeeding that may result in the puppy's becoming too heavy for his immature bone structure. Maintain the nutritive balance of the food. Use food additives only as directed, and only in the amounts directed.

As soon as possible after you get your puppy, have your veterinarian check him over and arrange for the protective shots against distemper, hepatitis, and leptospirosis (rabies shots come later in most cases). Your breeder should have given you the record of whatever puppy shots have already been given and when. Most veterinarians will recommend annual booster shots; "permanent shots" is a misnomer.

Your veterinarian will be the best judge of some of the more unusual things to check for in your puppy. Specifically, he will probably be examining the puppy for cataracts, umbilical hernia, undescended testicles or vaginal discharge, deafness, and internal parasites (for this, go prepared with a fresh stool specimen), as well as for the ordinary indications of good general health.

Most breeders will accept the return of a puppy that does not pass your veterinarian's examination satisfactorily, but be sure that you have this guarantee when you buy the puppy, preferably in writing.

Ten-week-old puppies. Clean puppies and clean kennel show the breeder cares.

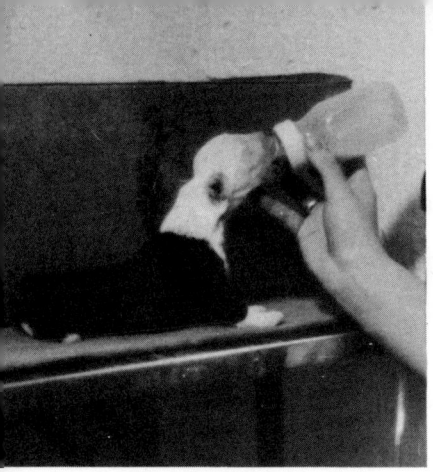

Week-old puppy owned by Dr. and Mrs. Sheldon Rennert.

Daily record of weight should be kept for each puppy. Failure to maintain regular gain may be early sign of problem.

When the breeder registers a purebred litter with The American Kennel Club, he receives for each puppy a form entitling it to be individually registered. This form is commonly known as the "blue slip." You should receive the slip, dated and signed by the breeder, when you buy your puppy.

When you have made two name choices and entered them on the front of the slip, mail it together with the fee to the AKC. Be sure that your name, address, and signature as the new owner are shown correctly on the reverse side. You will receive in return your puppy's registration certificate bearing whichever name was approved by the AKC.

If the puppy had already been issued an individual certificate, the breeder should date it and sign it over to you, and you should complete the form on the back, sign it, and send it with the fee to the AKC to transfer ownership. In this case, you have no choice of registered name because one has already been registered for him.

Weaning days—five and a half weeks.

Weaning four-week-old puppy with first taste of pablum—can be a messy (but fun!) job for the youngsters.

Four-week-old puppy gets wash-up after his pablum.

Sometimes the breeder has not yet received the blue slip or the certificate from the AKC, and he may promise to send it to you later. In this event, you must get a signed bill of sale from him clearly identifying your puppy as to breeder's name, sire and dam with their registration numbers, and the birth date of the puppy. Do not buy any puppy without receiving either the papers or the proper bill of sale with promise of papers to follow, if you want to have your puppy registered. Contact the AKC with the information if you do not receive the promised papers from the breeder.

With many owners, one Old English Sheepdog has led to more. If the prospect of having more than one tempts you, give long and serious thought to the question of whether or not you are really prepared to keep up the grooming and health of more than one of them over a long period of years. The average adult Sheepdog lives to be at least ten years of age, and many are still active at fourteen and more years.

Licking up the last—five weeks.

The household OES usually prefers a cold floor, linoleum or stone, to a warm carpet. Litter sisters Deardre's Shaggy Copy Cat and Amr/Can Ch. Deardre's Play It Again Shaggy, CD. Owners, Dr. and Mrs. Sheldon Rennert.

The Adult Old English Sheepdog

The intriguing words used by his enthusiastic admirers to describe and characterize the Old English Sheepdog are practically endless, for he is without peer whether as a companion or worker. Often called "The Bob-Tail" or "The Bob-tailed Sheepdog," his nickname was earned by the fact that his tail is docked a few days after birth.

The Sheepdog is probably most notable for his picturesque shaggy appearance and bear-like movement; his happy, loving nature; the effusive friendly greeting he accords to friend and stranger alike; and his remarkable intelligence.

He can see well, despite the thick fall of hair over his face, for on the move his hair blows back to give him an unobstructed view; at rest, strong wiry hairs hold the fall away from his eyes so that he misses nothing worth investigating. The oft-told tale that to remove the hair from over his eyes will cause him to go blind is simply not true.

While he is a strong, agile, fast-growing dog, reaching nearly his full height around eight or nine months in most cases, he continues to mature in a number of ways until he is two years old and even more. Full grown, the Sheepdog will weigh anywhere from sixty-five to seventy pounds in a small bitch to as much as a hundred twenty-five pounds in an unusually large, heavy male. I would think that the average one, however, would weigh somewhere between seventy and ninety pounds.

The normal healthy Sheepdog does better with regular exercise, at least a good daily walk and a frequent run in the open, but many adapt quite easily to a much less active life as apartment dwellers. A developmental routine of well-planned special exercise will be essential to keep the show dog in winning condition.

It is the fully-matured Sheepdog that is described in the Breed Standard adopted by the Old English Sheepdog Club of America, Inc., and approved by The American Kennel Club as the basis for judging at dog shows. The Standard has been worded substantially the same since its first pronouncement by the breed club in England in 1888.

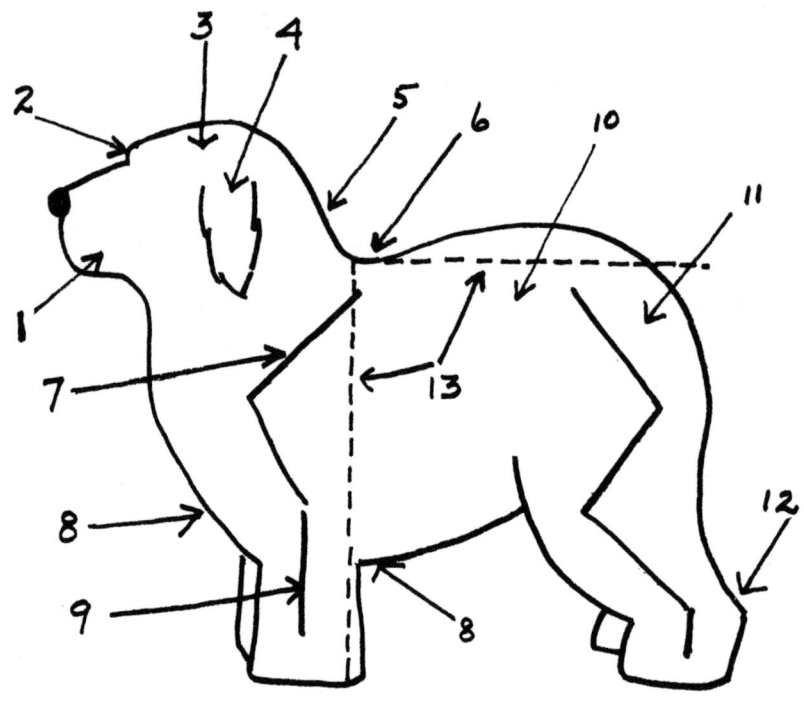

POINTS OF THE BREED STANDARD ILLUSTRATED
1. Jaw—fairly long, strong, square, truncated.
2. Stop—well-defined.
3. Skull—capacious, squarely formed.
4. Ears—set low enough to lie flat to head.
5. Neck—fairly long, arched gracefully.
6. Top shoulder points set close together.
7. Shoulder—sloping (45° angle).
8. Brisket—deep and capacious.
9. Forelegs—dead straight, large boned.
10. Loin higher than shoulders, stout and gently arched.
11. Hindquarters—round and muscular.
12. Hocks—well-let-down (close to ground).
13. Measurement—height measured withers to ground, about the same as body length from withers to rear, giving dog a square or compact appearance. Symmetry and soundness are emphasized.

The Standard for the Old English Sheepdog

(Reprinted with permission of the Old English Sheepdog Club of America, Inc.)

Skull—Capacious and rather squarely formed, giving plenty of room for brain power. The parts over the eyes should be well arched and the whole well covered with hair. *Jaw*—Fairly long, strong, square and truncated. The stop should be well defined to avoid a Deerhound face. (The attention of judges is particularly called to the above properties, as a long, narrow head is a deformity.) *Eyes*—Vary according to the color of the dog. Very dark preferred, but in the glaucous or blue dogs a pearl, walleye or china eye is considered typical. (A light eye is most objectionable.) *Nose*—Always black, large and capacious. *Teeth*—Strong and large, evenly placed and level in opposition. *Ears*—Medium-sized, and carried flat to side of head, coated moderately.

Legs—The forelegs should be dead straight, with plenty of bone, removing the body a medium height from the ground, without approaching legginess, and well coated all around. *Feet*—Small, round; toes well arched, and pads thick and hard. *Tail*—It is preferable that there should be none. Should never, however, exceed 1-½ or 2 inches in grown dogs. When not natural-born bobtails however, puppies should be docked at the first joint from the body and the operation performed when they are from three to four days old.

Neck and Shoulders—The neck should be fairly long, arched gracefully and well coated with hair. The shoulders sloping and narrow at the points, the dog standing lower at the shoulder than at the loin.

Body—Rather short and very compact, ribs well sprung and brisket deep and capacious. *Slabsidedness highly undesirable.* The loin should be very stout and gently arched, while the hindquarters should be round and muscular and with well-let-down hocks, and the hams densely coated with a thick, long jacket in excess of any other part.

Coat—Profuse, but not so excessive as to give the impression of the dog being overfat, and of a good hard texture; not straight, but shaggy and free from curl. *Quality and texture of coat to be considered above mere profuseness.* Softness or flatness of coat to be considered a fault. The undercoat should be a waterproof pile, when not removed by grooming or season.

Color—Any shade of gray, grizzle, blue or blue-merled with or without white markings or in reverse. *Any shade of brown or fawn to be considered distinctly objectionable and not to be encouraged.*

Size—Twenty-two inches and upwards for dogs and slightly less for bitches. Type, character and symmetry are of the greatest importance and are on no account to be sacrificed to size alone.

General Appearance and Characteristics—A strong, compact-looking dog of great symmetry, practically the same in measurement from shoulder to stern as in height, absolutely free from legginess or weaseness, very elastic in his gallop, but in walking or trotting he has a characteristic ambling or pacing movement, and his bark should be loud, with a peculiar "pot-casse" ring in it. Taking him all round, he is a profusely, but not *excessively* coated, thick-set, muscular, able-bodied dog with a most intelligent expression, free from all Poodle or Deerhound character. *Soundness should be considered of greatest importance.*

Scale of Points

Skull	5	Body and loins	10
Eyes	5	Hindquarters	10
Ears	5	Legs	10
Teeth	5	Coat (texture, quality and condition)	15
Nose	5		
Jaw	5	General appearance and movement	15
Foreface	5		
Neck and Shoulders	5	Total	100

(Approved October 13, 1953)

One problem with judging by the Standard is the varying interpretations of its meanings. For the beginner, at least, many parts of it seem general and even rather vaguely worded; and to people unfamiliar with dogs, some of its terms may even be incomprehensible. For instance, how narrow is "narrow," how large is "large," how *much* less is "slightly" less, and what is meant by the term "stop?" As this goes to press, the OESCA is in process of drafting a clarification (not a revision) of the Standard for the guidance of fanciers and judges.

The breeding and selection of the Sheepdog that best conforms to the Standard is an art and not an exact science. There *are* no *exact* measurements, and this is where experience in the study of a number of the best individuals is the best teacher.

Through the years certain aspects of the Standard from time to time get special emphasis as breeders seem to stress this or that. For example, a number of years ago, if one can judge by the pictures of top-winning dogs of the time, one might have observed that top lines looked uniformly too level. Apparently the problem was recognized and corrected. About ten years ago, the problem most emphasized by many breeders was alignment of bite. More recently, breeders seem to be concerned with getting more length of neck. Now, from what I have been observing in the ring, I should not be surprised if we began to have more concern expressed over getting lower hocks. And that is the way it goes—first this and then that gets out of balance, and breeders respond by giving special attention to the problem. Of course the difficulty with such concentration on particular areas is that one may lose sight of the requirement for overall symmetry and structural balance.

The Sheepdog begins life as a short-haired, black-and-white puppy whose coat seems to grow almost as fast as he does. The first coat is a single one and is quite soft, perhaps almost like velvet to the touch.

Beginning at about six to nine months of age (sometimes sooner, often somewhat later), his coat gradually turns gray, possibly very light in tone, starting usually around his shoulders. Gradually his entire dark coat disappears and you may find that he is also getting the soft, warm undercoat. Just when the undercoat appears may depend in part on the season of the year. The long, harsh adult coat then appears more gradually, perhaps noticeable first around the shoulders. With the full adult coat, by the time the dog is two or three years old he will probably look darker again; some will retain more of the grizzle-gray color than others. The white areas, of course, remain white throughout the coat change, but the adult white coat, too, will be of the harsher texture.

In a small minority of cases I have found that the light-colored period is extremely short, coming and going nearly unnoticed, and these may be the darker adults.

It is during the course of his coat changes that the Sheepdog presents the greatest problem to the groomer, for not only is he throwing puppy coat, but also some of the soft, new undercoat, all of which tangles and mats into the long coat and sometimes can become "felted" to the skin if overlooked. The groomer is in deep trouble if he has been unaware of the progressive change and has continued to do only a quick brush-up without taking the care to brush properly clear to the skin all over.

As with any breed, there are some particular problems associated generally with the Old English Sheepdog. Fortunately, aside from the obvious one of keeping up proper coat care, they are relatively few, if you don't count the ones (such as parasites and diseases) to be found in all dogs.

The most important problem to avoid in the adult, and one that can seldom be recognized at sight (at least by the novice), is Hip Dysplasia, often abbreviated as HD. Defined as a "neuromuscular disease," it might more aptly (from the layman's point of view) be termed a condition.

The disease begins, according to one report, with the failure of a nerve to the pectineus muscle, which then fails to hold the hip socket assembly in the proper position. The result is an abnormality in the structure of the hip (a secondary effect of the "disease") wherein the head of the long leg bone (the femur) does not fit tightly and properly into the hip socket (acetabulum). In many cases the acetabulum is found to be unusually shallow.

Depending on the degree of displacement in a given case, and perhaps on the strain exerted by the activity of the affected dog,

Sheepdog with coat clipped short—a view of what is underneath. This is a heavy—even overweight—specimen.

the loose fit (subluxation) of the bones may sooner or later cause an alteration in their shape at the points of wear, and the subsequent arthritic changes that occur will progressively aggravate the condition. HD occurs in all breeds of dogs that weigh about twenty-five pounds or more and grow rapidly during their early months; it occurs, but more rarely, in some of the smaller breeds.

The condition can affect the dog's movement, especially in his later years when the arthritis may cause a painful and severe limp.

Relatively few of the affected dogs, however, show any marked outward sign of its presence, at least until an advanced age, but if they are bred, their offspring run a high risk of being affected, too. In most cases HD cannot be diagnosed except in the adult, and then only by x-ray of the hips, normally done under anaesthetic.

Hip Dysplasia is believed to be inherited through a combination of genes (a "polygenic" factor), and it develops in the individual as the puppy grows, some cases eventually becoming more severe than others. Since it is considered to be inherited, conscientious breeders use for breeding only x-rayed stock that has been found to have "normal" hips. Buying an adult Sheepdog rather than a puppy, one has a better chance of getting a dog that will remain free of HD because an x-ray will reveal the condition, whereas in the young puppy the condition has not yet developed and x-raying is premature. HD does occur, though less frequently, in dogs whose sire and dam were x-rayed and found to be "clear" of the condition.

If you cannot find a local veterinarian equipped to do x-rays properly, and if a veterinary school is not too far away, you can rely on the school's radiologists to take good-quality x-rays in the correct position. Many breeders prefer to leave the diagnosis (for a fee) to the Orthopedic Foundation for Animals (O.F.A.) located at the Veterinary School of the University of Missouri at Columbia, where a panel of qualified radiologists confers on each x-ray submitted and furnishes an evaluation statement. They will issue a numbered certificate for dogs found to have "normal" hips at a minimum age of two years, but they will also evaluate x-rays taken before the dog is two years of age.

The adult Sheepdog should be examined and certified by a veterinary ophthalmologist as free of any sign of eye disease or defect, particularly as to any of the major ocular diseases that are congenital and inheritable, such as Progressive Retinal Atrophy, Central PRA, and cataracts.

You will naturally avoid the dog with a thin, scraggly, or motheaten-looking coat, and you will look for the one with the best coarse texture to the long outer coat. Don't stop there, however. Closely examine the skin condition underneath the coat.

Eczema or "hot spots" is a fairly common problem in the Sheepdog and is possibly related in some degree, at least, to the fact that he has the sort of coat that he has. The problem can occur at any season of the year and in any climate. In many cases, I believe, it stems initially from the presence of fleas or ticks and

Puppy playpen pals.

the scratching and irritation (even infection) that follow. Other opinion holds that dry skin is the primary cause, and some owners rely, apparently with notable success, on supplementary feeding of fats or corn oils as a preventive measure.

In any case, frequent and thorough grooming should do much to keep the coat and skin healthy and free of parasites, and to reveal trouble spots early enough for the prompt treatment that can prevent more severe involvements. Examine promptly any areas that the dog scratches or bites at repeatedly. Inflamed areas should be brought to the attention of your veterinarian without delay.

The most effective treatment for eczema that I have used is an old remedy prescribed by my veterinarian. A liquid drying agent daubed on the affected areas twice daily, it is a combination of tannic acid and salicylic acid in an alcohol base. In severe cases a cortisone shot can help alleviate the inflammation and itching, and if treatment has been delayed too long, antibiotics may be indicated. Early discovery followed by prompt and faithful treatment usually prevents all but a minimum loss of coat.

I have never known a Sheepdog that I thought was naturally mean or bad tempered, and temperament has not so far been a par-

Proper OES movement showing correct timing, good reach forward and back, head up.

ticular concern in the breed. However, indiscriminate breeding prompted by the growing popularity of the breed has been said by some persons to be introducing more widely some of the less-desirable canine traits, so I would not be unduly surprised to hear occasionally of a case of bad temperament in a Sheepdog. I would still suspect, though, that a number of even those few cases would have been the result of poor training or early mistreatment rather than of anything else. If the playful puppy that nips and bites, especially during his teething days, is not trained to keep his teeth out of his games, he may well grow up with the idea that biting is acceptable; the result is that he will be accused of "meanness" or of having a "bad temperament."

Avoid the excessively shy or nervous dog that seemingly takes too cautiously to a stranger or who patently avoids his owner's hands and cringes from your touch. Do not reject the one that barks at your approach to his property, so long as he accepts your friendly overtures readily. With his sensitive hearing and characteristic bark, the Sheepdog makes an excellent watchdog, but he is not a natural guard dog in any but the most threatening circumstances.

Old English Sheepdogs owned by Ken and Meg Crump.

Ch. Pinafore Captain Gruntz, CDX, in a pin-up. Tying up the Sheepdog's head coat does not injure the eyes; in fact, it helps him to see. Some dogs object to it, however.

Getting out the last bit of cornstarch at Westminster with admiring onlookers. Serena Van Rensselaer and Ch. Fezziwig Raggedy Andy shortly before "Andy" took Group First at his last Westminster Show.

Grooming the Old English Sheepdog for Show

Proper care of the Sheepdog's coat is essential to his comfort, health, and appearance. The process of grooming the dog is basically the same whether for routine maintenance or for showing; the only difference is the method and direction of the final brush-up for the ring.

The puppy with the soft, short, single coat that is so simple to keep brushed up with an ordinary bristle brush in five minutes a day, can seemingly overnight become the full-sized nine-month-old with a longer outer coat and a tangled, matted undercoat that defies brush and comb. Usually the source of the trouble is the short, soft undercoat (especially in a time of seasonal shedding), which mats and becomes tangled in the outer coat. It will be important to keep the dog groomed thoroughly and regularly in order to prevent the problem. It is small consolation at the time to know that after he is about three years old and has his full adult coat, routine maintenance will be somewhat less troublesome except, again, during seasonal shedding in the early spring and fall.

There are few professionals able and willing to groom a Sheepdog properly, and few owners can afford the fees of those who will; so it usually means you must learn to do the grooming yourself or else keep the dog clipped short (which doesn't present exactly the pretty picture one associates with the breed). The best way to learn the technique is to arrange one or two live demonstrations by an experienced hand.

The Equipment. Begin by investing in the proper equipment of the best quality. The best combs and brushes will last for years; you will soon become dissatisfied with cheaper products. Avoid falling for the highly-advertised item that promises to make grooming an effortless undertaking. The razor-like "mat splitter" is never necessary and is dangerous to groomer and dog alike, especially in inexperienced hands. The "fuss-free, scientifically-designed" rake-comb whose "heavy-duty metal teeth glide through mats, knots, and burs easily and painlessly" is not for the Sheepdog because it promises far more than it can deliver.

You should by all means invest in a grooming table at the very beginning, preferably a folding one, on which the dog will lie at a comfortable working height. A table can be purchased at a pet supply house or, if you are handy, you can construct a table similar to the one shown on page 36. Sturdy folding legs can be purchased for your homemade table.

Though the coat of the young puppy normally presents no difficulty, it is during this early, easy period that he should be trained to enjoy the grooming process in preparation for the longer sessions he must undergo later. The dog will come to enjoy the attention and owner contact that grooming offers, and he may even go to sleep while you work away on him. With patience and gentle reassurance, start early to train him to lie on his side for grooming.

The large pin-brush will be your principal routine grooming tool, with an assist at times from the comb. The latter is used primarily to remove larger mats and at such tricky or sensitive spots as around and on the ears, chin, and eyes. When done in conjunction with a fine mist spray of water, very dilute creme rinse, or the coat conditioner of your choice, brushing serves to clean the coat as well as to keep it free of mats and debris.

How to Proceed. The one key to proper grooming is to brush the coat TO THE SKIN EVERYWHERE. There is never any shortcut to the job of grooming a full-coated Sheepdog except to do the job right, with regularity, and frequently enough that severe difficulties do not develop. The frequency of grooming required will depend so much on the season, the climate, the age of the dog, and the characteristics and habits of the individual dog, that any generalization about it would be misleading.

With the dog stretched out comfortably on his side, begin by parting a line on the coat either lengthwise or vertically on his side. Where to start is not important; eventually you will do the entire side and as far around the body as possible everywhere.

Using long, slow strokes from the skin outward to the tip of the hair, brush thoroughly and gently along the entire part line until the brush meets no resistance anywhere. Most people prefer to brush in the direction that the coat grows, holding back with the other hand the ungroomed coat on the opposite side of the part line. The stroke should be a lifting and fluffing one, *not* one where the hair is brushed down flat as one might brush over the surface of the human head of hair. Continue to brush in this manner, progressively separating the hair in a new part line close to the section just completed as you proceed over the entire side.

Loose undercoat is removed at any small stubborn areas by carefully teasing and brushing it out with shorter strokes to preserve as much coat as possible. The comb should be reserved for use on only the larger and more stubborn mats. In some cases the "slicker brush" is helpful to prevent future matting by removing the very tiny pills of loose undercoat. The slicker does remove more undercoat than the pin-brush and is therefore not favored by show groomers in most cases.

For large mats, use the comb vertically (at right angles to the skin) through the mat to separate it into manageable sections. You can also attack a large mat effectively by working gradually from one side of it with the comb, cleaning it out a few hairs at a time as you proceed across the whole mat.

It is more comfortable for the dog at difficult areas if you use one hand to hold the mat between the comb and the skin, teasing out the matted loose coat a little at a time, beginning to clear out the tip of the coat first and gradually working in toward the skin.

With the dog on the same side, groom out the uppermost side of all four legs, again using the brush for as much of the job as possible. Most people find it easier to begin at the foot and work gradually upward, holding the ungroomed coat up out of the way as they proceed. Then turn the dog over and repeat the process on the other side.

The Feet. On the bottom of the feet, carefully trim with small scissors as much hair as possible from between the pads. Blunt-tipped scissors with sharp, slightly-curved blades make the best tool for this. The close trimming helps to keep the foot clean and free of foreign objects that can otherwise become entangled in the hair, giving the dog pain in movement or causing the feet to spread out. Finish by clipping the nails as necessary and filing off sharp edges as described on page 35.

The Ears. No grooming session should end until the ears are examined and the accumulated wax removed, using rubbing alcohol on cotton balls as far into the canal as you can easily reach with your finger. (The canal goes generally in a forward and slightly downward direction on the dog's head.) Pull all hair from the canal and outer ear (not from the ear flap). If you cannot pull the hair with your fingers, use a hemostat, removing only a few hairs at a time. Consult your veterinarian promptly if you find a bad odor, an inflamed condition, or an abnormal discharge. As a precaution, some owners use an antibiotic ointment in the ear after each such cleaning.

Bathing. Cornstarch can be used effectively to clean white portions of the coat. Dampen the coat with a fine spray of water. With the fingers, thoroughly rub in generous portions of cornstarch (it can be sprinkled on with a large-holed kitchen salt shaker). Allow to dry briefly and vigorously brush it out of the coat. For the show ring, be sure it is *all* brushed out.

Ordinarily, little bathing is required for the Sheepdog unless a special tick or flea treatment is necessary. For extra whiteness, show dogs are usually bathed on the white portions of the legs a few days before a show. A bath tends to soften the coat texture temporarily, so it is usually not undertaken immediately prior to showing. Any bathing, however, should be done only *after* the coat has first been brushed entirely free of mats and debris.

In most circumstances, the long outer coat of the adult acts as a waterproof protection, and after a few hours, what dried mud does not drop off the coat can easily be brushed off, leaving the coat white again. In case of a dip in salt water, muddy pond, or chlorinated pool, however, a thorough rinse-off with the garden hose is advisable.

It takes a lot of water and a lot of lathering to get down to the skin on a Sheepdog, and "once over lightly" may leave the skin untouched with even the water. If a bath is necessary, follow the procedure described on pages 34 and 35 for bathing the family dog.

After bathing, towel the coat partially dry without rubbing in such a way as to tangle the coat. Handfuls of coat can be squeezed with the towel like a sponge. Then the dog can be allowed to finish drying naturally or his appearance can be enhanced by brushing him dry (the use of an electric hair dryer as you are brushing is a big help). Cover the table under him with a beach towel as you dry the first side. Remove the towel to do his other side, and his dry side will not be dampened again by a wet table.

Trimming for Show. Much more scissor trimming, shaping, and sculpturing has been done in recent years, especially in some areas of the country, than was commonly done a few years ago to prepare the Sheepdog for the show ring. Apparently the intent has been to make the dog's appearance conform more closely to some extreme conception of the ideal described in the Standard. It seems fairly certain now, however, that such practices will no longer be so common. In October of 1975 the Old English Sheepdog Club of America voted to "go on record as opposing the extreme trimming and sculpturing of the Old English Sheepdog, altering the Old English Sheepdog coat by sprays, and presenting the

Old English Sheepdog at excessive speeds in the show ring,'' and to inform the breed judges of that fact.

Different dogs will present different problems in appearance which judicious brushing or some minor and hardly discernible scissoring can improve—for example, the dog whose rear legs are too close together, the one that is too long in body or too low in the rear, the one with a short neck, and so on. However, these special "tricks of the trade," which may fool the spectators but seldom the judge, are not the show trimming procedures that will be described here.

With the dog standing, the coat on the feet should be trimmed off at the bottom all around about even with the floor. The purpose here is to retain the rugged, shaggy appearance without leaving coat to drag in the dust or straggle out in all directions and mop up the floor. Ideally, the front legs should give the impression of straight-sided pedestals.

For cleanliness and ease of daily care, the hair surrounding the anus of *all* Sheepdogs should be clipped off as short as possible, the extent of the clipped area depending somewhat on how much long hair from above will naturally fall over and conceal it (primarily a question of aesthetics).

For my own dogs, which are no longer exhibited, I prefer also to even up and shorten the coat slightly on and around the rear to emphasize the rounded effect and to eliminate some of the long fall down behind. When the coat is then brushed outward in a circle from about the tail area, it will hold the brushed shape.

The scissoring on the rear is done with the scissor blades always *pointing down,* removing only very small amounts each time, while the coat is brushed downward from the top line. When the scissors are used to cut either upward or across the fall, the dog may end up looking as if he backed into a fan or was sliced off at the back end like a loaf of bread, which is not proper for the Sheepdog, though it once commonly appeared in the ring in some areas.

However, since all sculpturing or trimming has recently met with such strong opposition among fanciers and has been condemned by the breed club, even this much trimming may soon be penalized by the judges.

The coat over the eyes can obstruct the dog's view when it has been freshly groomed, and as a result he may not keep his head up properly when moving. Some handlers do a minimum of back-combing over the eyes, which may be helpful, but the use of a holding hair spray, either to hold up the eye coat or to give a spurious

Welcome! A groomer's challenge! This mud is on the surface only. Underneath, the dog remains fairly clean despite appearances.

Same muddy dog groomed.

texture to the coat, is not permitted under AKC dog show rules and is condemned by the breed club.

Under present rules the coat over the Sheepdog's eyes may not be tied up for the obedience ring, but the breed club is trying to persuade the AKC to relax this rule for obedience. The Sheepdog is occasionally seen in the obedience ring with his coat clipped off short all over, which seems to be acceptable and which certainly solves the problem of his ability to see in performing the exercises for the Open and Utility Classes.

Final Brushing Pattern. While the general picture of the Sheepdog in the ring is one of a shaggy dog whose coat stands out from

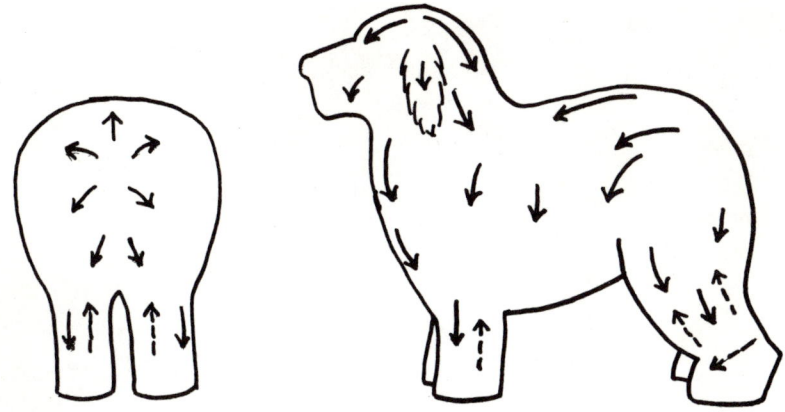

Pattern for final brushing for show. Solid-line arrows indicate first brushing before fluffing. Dotted-line arrows indicate direction of final fluffing on legs. Coat should be fluffed all over to stand out from body; this will also blend areas where direction of brushings meet conflicting direction. Cross-brushing at hocks emphasizes low hocks.

the body everywhere as much as possible, the coat is brushed (and then fluffed out) in different directions on different parts of the body, mostly in the direction of its natural growth or fall.

Usually the brushing pattern is forward and down on the head and face from the crown; back and down on the neck, chest and sides; forward on the top line from the rear to the shoulders; upward on the legs; outward in a circle from a point on the back end just below the tail area. Obviously there will be points where one direction of brushing comes up against an opposite direction, but these points will blend satisfactorily when the light touch of the brush is used for the blending and the final fluffing effect.

Kiddie pool in backyard serves as tub for bath. Attire of groomers should be appropriate for the occasion.

"Penny" is not too enthusiastic about the procedure but submits to the indignity obediently—and with no little embarrassment

In rough coat—not trimmed for show—fresh from a quick dry after a bath.

a puppy, extreme care must be exercised so that he will not become chilled. No dog should be bathed during cold weather and then permitted to go outside immediately. Whatever the weather, the dog should always be given a good run outdoors and permitted to relieve himself before he is bathed.

Various types of "dry baths" are available, and in general, they are quite satisfactory when circumstances are such that a bath in water is impractical. Dry shampoos are usually worked into the dog's coat thoroughly, then removed by towelling or brushing.

Before starting a water bath, the necessary equipment should be assembled. This includes a tub of appropriate size, preferably one that has a drain so that the water will not accumulate and the dog will not be kept standing in water throughout the bath. A rubber mat should be placed in the bottom of the tub to prevent the dog from slipping. A small hose with a spray nozzle—one that may be attached to the water faucet—is ideal for wetting and rinsing the coat, but if such equipment is not available, then a second tub or a large pail should be provided for bath and rinse water. A metal or plastic cup for dipping water, special dog shampoo, a small bottle of mineral or olive oil, and a supply of absorbent cotton should be placed nearby, as well as a supply of heavy towels, a wash cloth, and the dog's combs and brushes. Bath water and rinse water should be slightly warmer than lukewarm, but should not be hot.

To avoid accidentally getting water in the dog's ears, place a small amount of absorbent cotton in each. With the dog standing in the tub, wet his body by using the hose and spray nozzle or by using the cup to pour water over him. Take care to avoid wetting the head, and be careful to avoid getting water or shampoo in the eyes. (If you should accidentally do so, placing a few drops of mineral or olive oil in the inner corner of the eye will bring relief.) When the dog is thoroughly wet, put a small amount of shampoo on his back and work the lather into the coat with a gentle, squeezing action. Wash the entire body and then use the cup and container of water (or hose and spray nozzle) to rinse the dog thoroughly.

Dip the wash cloth into clean water, wring it out enough so it won't drip, then wash the dog's head, taking care to avoid the eyes. Remove the cotton from the dog's ears and sponge them gently, inside and out. Shampoo should never be used inside the ears, so if they are extremely soiled, sponge them clean with cotton saturated with mineral or olive oil. (Between baths, the ears should be cleaned frequently in the same way.)

Grooming the Family Dog

Every dog should be taught from puppyhood that a grooming session is a time for business, not for play. He should be handled gently, though, for it is essential to avoid hurting him in any way. Grooming time should be pleasant for both dog and master.

A light, airy, pleasant place in which to work is desirable, and it is of the utmost importance that neither dog nor master be distracted by other dogs, cats, or people. Consequently, it is usually preferable that grooming be done indoors.

Before each session, the dog should be permitted to relieve himself. Once grooming is begun, it is important to avoid keeping the dog standing so long that he becomes tired. If a good deal of grooming is needed, it should be done in two or more short periods.

A sturdy grooming table is desirable. The dog should stand on the grooming table while the back and upper portions of his body are groomed, and lie on his side while underparts of his body are brushed, nails clipped, etc.

It is almost impossible to brush too much, and show dogs are often brushed for a full half hour a day, year round. If you cannot brush your dog every day, you should brush him a minimum of two or three times a week. Brushing removes loose skin particles and stimulates circulation, thereby improving condition of the skin. I also stimulates secretion of the natural skin oils that make the co look healthy and beautiful.

Before brushing, any burs adhering to the coat, as well as mat hair, should be carefully removed, using the fingers and coa toothed comb with a gentle, teasing motion to avoid tearing coat. The coat should first be brushed lightly in the directic which the hair grows. Next, it should be brushed in the opp direction, a small portion at a time, making sure the bristles trate the hair to the skin, until the entire coat has been br thoroughly and all loose soil removed. Then the coat sho brushed in the direction the hair grows, until every hair is sl place.

The dog that is kept well brushed needs bathing onl Once or twice a year is usually enough. If it is necessary

Quickly wrap a towel around the dog, remove him from the tub, and towel him as dry as possible. To avoid getting an impromptu bath yourself, you must act quickly, for once he is out of the tub, the dog will instinctively shake himself.

While the hair is still slightly damp, use a clean comb or brush to remove any tangles. If the hair is allowed to dry first, it may be completely impossible to remove them.

So far as routine grooming is concerned, the dog's eyes require little attention. Some dogs have a slight accumulation of mucus in the corner of the eyes upon waking mornings. A salt solution (a teaspoon of table salt to one pint of warm, sterile water) can be sponged around the eyes to remove the stain. During grooming sessions it is well to inspect the eyes, since many breeds are prone to eye injury. Eye problems of a minor nature may be treated at home (see page 54), but it is imperative that any serious eye abnormality be called to the attention of the veterinarian immediately.

Feeding hard dog biscuits and hard bones helps to keep tooth surfaces clean. Slight discoloration may be readily removed by rubbing with a damp cloth dipped in salt or baking soda. The dog's head should be held firmly, the lips pulled apart gently, and the teeth rubbed lightly with the dampened cloth. Regular care usually keeps the teeth in good condition, but if tartar accumulates, it should be removed by a veterinarian.

If the dog doesn't keep his nails worn down through regular exercise on hard surfaces, they must be trimmed at intervals, for nails that are too long may cause the foot to spread and thus spoil the dog's gait. Neglected nails may even grow so long that they will grow into a circle and puncture the dog's skin. Nails can be cut easily with any of the various types of nail trimmers. The cut is made just outside the faintly pink bloodline that can be seen on white nails. In pigmented nails, the bloodline is not easily seen, so the cut should be made just outside the hooklike projection on the underside of the nails. A few downward strokes with a nail file will smooth the cut surface, and, once shortened, nails can be kept short by filing at regular intervals.

Care must be taken that nails are not cut too short, since blood vessels may be accidentally severed. Should you accidentally cut a nail so short that it bleeds, apply a mild antiseptic and keep the dog quiet until bleeding stops. Usually, only a few drops of blood will be lost. But once a dog's nails have been cut painfully short, he will usually object when his feet are handled.

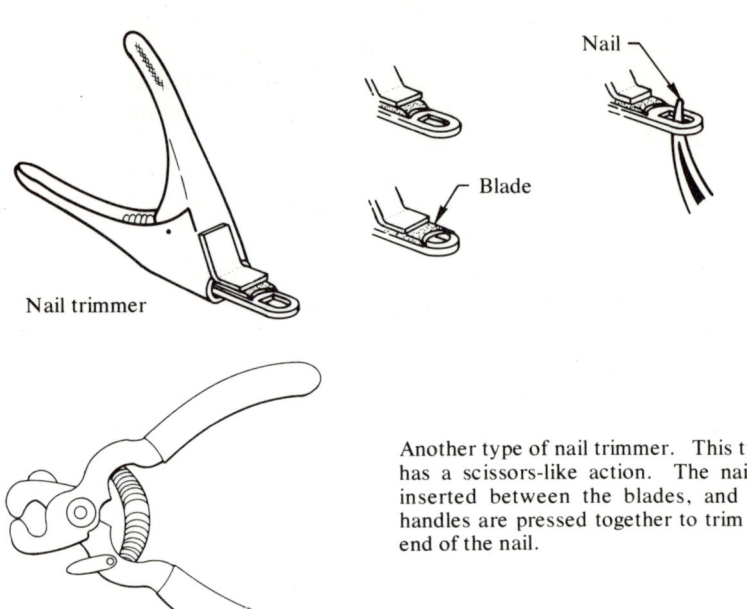

Another type of nail trimmer. This type has a scissors-like action. The nail is inserted between the blades, and the handles are pressed together to trim the end of the nail.

Dog crate with grooming-table top provides rigid, well supported surface on which to groom dog, and serves as indoor kennel for puppy or grown dog. Rubber matting provides non-slip surface. Dog's collar may be attached to adjustable arm.

Centered below is a grooming table with an adjustable arm to which the dog's collar may be attached. The adjustable arm at right below may be clamped to an ordinary table or other rigid surface which will serve as a grooming table.

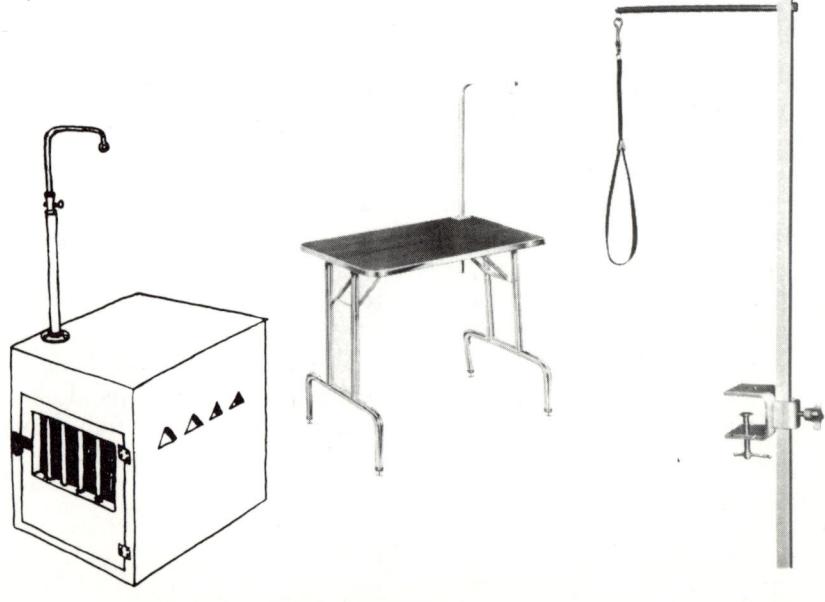

"Bed and Board" for the Family Dog

It is much easier to adapt to the demands of a new puppy if you collect the necessary equipment before you bring him home. You will need a water and food dish—preferably stainless steel and of a type that will not tip easily. You will need some chew toys, a soft puppy lead, and a soft hair brush for puppy grooming. You will need to decide where your dog is going to sleep and to prepare his bed.

Every dog should have a bed of his own, snug and warm, where he can retire undisturbed when he wishes to nap. And, especially with a small puppy, it is desirable to have the bed arranged so the dog can be securely confined at times, safe and contented. If the puppy is taught early in life to stay quietly in his box at night, or when the family is out, the habit will carry over into adulthood and will benefit both dog and master.

The dog should never be banished to a damp, cold basement, but should be quartered in an out-of-the-way corner close to the center of family activity. His bed can be an elaborate cushioned affair with electric warming pad, or simply a rectangular wooden box or heavy paper carton, cushioned with a clean cotton rug or towel. Actually, the latter is ideal for a new puppy, for it is snug, easy to clean, and expendable. A "door" can be cut on one side of the box for easy access, but it should be placed in such a way that the dog can still be confined when desirable.

The shipping crates used by professional handlers at dog shows make ideal indoor quarters. They are lightweight but strong, provide adequate air circulation, yet are snug and warm and easily cleaned. For the dog owner who takes his dog along when he travels, a dog crate is ideal, for the dog will willingly stay in his accustomed bed during long automobile trips, and the crate can be taken inside motels or hotels at night, making the dog a far more acceptable guest.

Dog crates are made of chromed metal or wood, and some have tops covered with a special rubber matting so they can be used as grooming tables. Anyone moderately handy with tools can construct a crate similar to the one illustrated on the opposite page.

Crates come in various sizes, to suit various breeds of dogs. For reasons of economy, the size selected for a puppy should be adequate for use when the dog is full grown. If the area seems too large when the puppy is small, a temporary cardboard partition can be installed to limit the area he occupies.

For the owner's convenience and to enhance the dog's sense of security, food and water dishes may be kept in the same general area where the crate is kept.

Nutrition

The main food elements required by dogs are proteins, fats, and carbohydrates. Vitamins A, B complex, D, and E are essential, as are ample amounts of calcium and iron. Nine other minerals are required in small amounts but are amply provided in almost any diet, so there is no need to be concerned about them.

The most important nutrient is protein and it must be provided every day of the dog's life, for it is essential for normal daily growth and replacement of body tissues burned up in daily activity. Preferred animal protein products are beef, mutton, horse meat, and boned fish. Visceral organs—heart, liver, and tripe—are good but if used in too large quantities may cause diarrhea (bones in large amounts have the same effect). Some veterinarians feel that pork is undesirable, while others consider lean pork acceptable as long as it is well cooked. Bacon drippings are often recommended for inclusion in the dog's diet, but this is a matter best discussed with your veterinarian since the salt in the bacon drippings might prove harmful to a dog that is not in good health. The "meat meal" used in some commercial foods is made from scrap meat processed at high temperatures and then dried. It is not quite so nutritious as fresh meat, but in combination with other protein products, it is an acceptable ingredient in the dog's diet.

Cooked eggs and raw egg yolk are good sources of protein, but raw egg white should never be fed since it may cause diarrhea. Cottage cheese and milk (fresh, dried, and canned) are high in protein, also. Puppies thrive on milk and it is usually included in the diet until the puppy is about three months of age, but when fed to older dogs it often causes diarrhea. Soy-bean meal, wheat germ meal, and dried brewers yeast are vegetable products high in protein and may be used to advantage in the dog's diet.

Vegetable and animal fats in moderate amounts should be used, especially if a main ingredient of the diet is dry or kibbled food. Fats should not be used excessively or the dog may become overweight. Generally, fats should be increased slightly in the winter and reduced somewhat during warm weather.

Carbohydrates are required for proper assimilation of fats. Dog biscuits, kibble, dog meal, and other dehydrated foods are good sources of carbohydrates, as are cereal products derived from rice, corn, wheat, and ground or rolled oats.

Vegetables supply additional proteins, vitamins, and minerals, and by providing bulk are of value in overcoming constipation. Raw or cooked carrots, celery, lettuce, beets, asparagus, tomatoes, and cooked spinach may be used. They should always be chopped or ground well and mixed with the other food. Various combinations may be used, but a good home-mixed ration for the mature dog consists of two parts of meat and one each of vegetables and dog meal (or cereal product).

Dicalcium phosphate and cod-liver oil are added to puppy diets to ensure inclusion of adequate amounts of calcium and Vitamins A and D. Indiscriminate use of dietary supplements is not only unjustified but may be harmful and many breeders feel that their over-use may lead to excessive growth as well as to overweight at maturity. Also, kidney damage in adult dogs has been traced to over-supplementation of the diet with calcium and Vitamin D.

Foods manufactured by well-known and reputable food processors are nutritionally sound and are offered in sufficient variety of flavors, textures, and consistencies that most dogs will find them tempting and satisfying. Canned foods are usually "ready to eat," while dehydrated foods in the form of kibble, meal, or biscuits may require the addition of water or milk. Dried foods containing fat sometimes become rancid, so to avoid an unpalatable change in flavor, the manufacturer may not include fat in dried food but recommend its addition at the time the water or milk is added.

Candy and other sweets are taboo, for the dog has no nutritional need for them and if he is permitted to eat them, he will usually eat less of foods he requires. Also taboo are fried foods, highly seasoned foods, and extremely starchy foods, for the dog's digestive tract is not equipped to handle them.

Frozen foods should be thawed completely and warmed at least to lukewarm, while hot foods should be cooled to lukewarm. Food should be in a fairly firm state, for sloppy food is difficult for the dog to digest.

Whether meat is raw or cooked makes little difference, so long as the dog is also given the juice that seeps from the meat during cooking. Bones provide little nourishment, although gnawing bones helps make the teeth strong and helps to keep tartar from accumulating on them. Beef bones, especially large knuckle bones, are best. Fish, poultry, and chop bones should never be given to dogs since they have a tendency to splinter and may puncture the dog's digestive tract.

Clean, fresh, cool water is essential and an adequate supply should be available twenty-four hours a day from the time the puppy is big enough to walk. Especially during hot weather, the drinking pan should be emptied and refilled at frequent intervals.

Puppies usually are weaned by the time they are six weeks old, so when you acquire a new puppy ten to twelve weeks old, he will already have been started on a feeding schedule. The breeder should supply exact details as to number of meals per day, types and amounts of food offered, etc. It is essential to adhere to this established routine, for drastic changes in diet may produce intestinal upsets. In most instances, a combination of dry meal, canned meat, and the plastic wrapped hamburger-like products provide a well-balanced diet. For a puppy that is too fat or too thin, or for one that has health problems, a veterinarian may recommend a specially formulated diet, but ordinarily, the commercially prepared foods can be used.

The amount of food offered at each meal must gradually be increased and by five months the puppy will require about twice what he needed at three months. However, the puppy should not be allowed to become too fat. Obesity has become a major health problem for dogs, and it is estimated that forty-one percent of American dogs are overweight. It is essential that weight be controlled throughout the dog's lifetime and that the dog be kept in trim condition—neither too fat nor too thin—for many physical problems can be traced directly to overweight. If the habit of overeating is developed in puppyhood, controlling the weight of the mature dog will be much more difficult.

A mature dog usually eats slightly less than he did as a growing puppy. For mature dogs, one large meal a day is usually sufficient, although some owners prefer to give two meals. As long as the dog enjoys optimum health and is neither too fat nor too thin, the number of meals a day makes little difference.

The amount of food required for mature dogs will vary. With canned dog food or home-prepared foods (that is, the combination of meat, vegetables, and meal), the approximate amount required is one-half ounce of food per pound of body weight. If the dog is fed a dehydrated commercial food, approximately one ounce of food is needed for each pound of body weight. Most manufacturers of commercial foods provide information on packages as to approximate daily needs of various breeds.

For most dogs, the amount of food provided should be increased slightly during the winter months and reduced somewhat during hot weather when the dog is less active.

As a dog becomes older and less active, he may become too fat. Or his appetite may decrease so he becomes too thin. It is necessary to adjust the diet in either case, for the dog will live longer and enjoy better health if he is maintained in trim condition. The simplest way to decrease or increase body weight is by decreasing or increasing the amount of fat in the diet. Protein content should be maintained at a high level throughout the dog's life.

If the older dog becomes reluctant to eat, it may be necessary to coax him with special food he normally relishes. Warming the food will increase its aroma and usually will help to entice the dog to eat. If he still refuses, rubbing some of the food on the dog's lips and gums may stimulate interest. It may be helpful also to offer food in smaller amounts and increase the number of meals per day. Foods that are highly nutritious and easily digested are especially desirable for older dogs. Small amounts of cooked, ground liver, cottage cheese, or mashed, hard-cooked eggs should be included in the diet often.

Before a bitch is bred, her owner should make sure that she is in optimum condition—slightly on the lean side rather than fat. The bitch in whelp is given much the same diet she was fed prior to breeding, with slight increases in amounts of meat, liver, and dairy products. Beginning about six weeks after breeding, she should be fed two meals per day rather than one, and the total daily intake increased. (Some bitches in whelp require as much as 50% more food than they consume normally.) She must not be permitted to become fat, for whelping problems are more likely to occur in overweight dogs. Cod-liver oil and dicalcium phosphate should be provided until after the puppies are weaned.

The dog used only occasionally for breeding will not require a special diet, but he should be well fed and maintained in optimum condition. A dog used frequently may require a slightly increased amount of food. But his basic diet will require no change so long as his general health is good and his flesh is firm and hard.

Dishes of this type are available in both plastic and stainless steel.

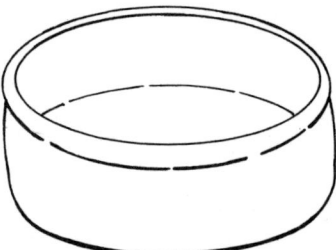

Crockery dish for food or water.

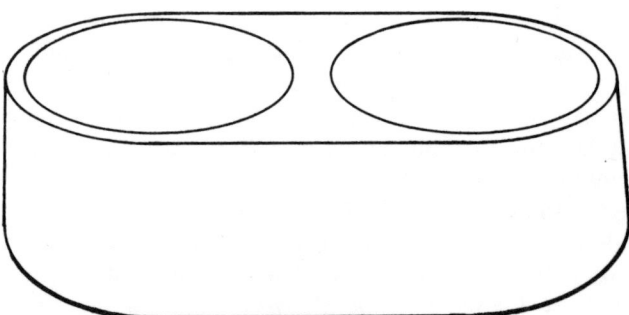

Stainless steel dish for food and water.

Maintaining the Dog's Health

In dealing with health problems, simple measures of preventive care are always preferable to cures—which may be complicated and costly. Many of the problems which afflict dogs can be avoided quite easily by instituting good dog-keeping practices in connection with feeding and housing.

Proper nutrition is essential in maintaining the dog's resistance to infectious diseases, in reducing susceptibility to organic diseases, and, of course, in preventing dietary deficiency diseases.

Cleanliness is essential in preventing the growth of disease-producing bacteria and other micro-organisms. All equipment, especially water and food dishes, must be kept immaculately clean. Cleanliness is also essential in controlling external parasites, which thrive in unsanitary surroundings.

Symptoms of Illness

Symptoms of illness may be so obvious there is no question that the dog is ill, or so subtle that the owner isn't sure whether there is a change from normal or not. **Loss of appetite, malaise** (general lack of interest in what is going on), **and vomiting** may be ignored if they occur singly and persist only for a day. However, in combination with other evidence of illness, such symptoms may be significant and the dog should be watched closely. **Abnormal bowel movements,** especially diarrhea or bloody stools, are causes for immediate concern. **Urinary abnormalities** may indicate infections, and bloody urine is always an indication of a serious condition. When a dog that has long been housebroken suddenly becomes incontinent, a veterinarian should be consulted, for he may be able to suggest treatment or medication that will be helpful.

Fever is a positive indication of illness and consistent deviation from the normal temperature range of 100 to 102 degrees is cause for concern. Have the dog in a standing position when taking his temperature. Coat the bulb of a rectal thermometer with petroleum jelly, raise the dog's tail, insert the thermometer to approximately half its length, and hold it in position for two minutes. Clean the thermometer with rubbing alcohol after each use and be sure to shake it down.

Fits, often considered a symptom of worms, may result from a variety of causes, including vitamin deficiencies, or playing to the point of exhaustion. A veterinarian should be consulted when a fit occurs, for it may be a symptom of serious illness.

Persistent coughing is often considered a symptom of worms, but may also indicate heart trouble—especially in older dogs.

Stary coat—dull and lackluster—indicates generally poor health and possible worm infestation. **Dull eyes** may result from similar conditions. Certain forms of blindness may also cause the eyes to lose the sparkle of vibrant good health.

Vomiting is another symptom often attributed to worm infestation. Dogs suffering from indigestion sometimes eat grass, apparently to induce vomiting and relieve discomfort.

Accidents and Injuries

Injuries of a serious nature—deep cuts, broken bones, severe burns, etc.—always require veterinary care. However, the dog may need first aid before being moved to a veterinary hospital.

A dog injured in any way should be approached cautiously, for reactions of a dog in pain are unpredictable and he may bite even a beloved master. A muzzle should always be applied before any attempt is made to move the dog or treat him in any way. The muzzle can be improvised from a strip of cloth, bandage, or even heavy cord, looped firmly around the dog's jaws and tied under the lower jaw. The ends should then be extended back of the neck and tied again so the loop around the jaws will stay in place.

A stretcher for moving a heavy dog can be improvised from a rug or board, and preferably two people should be available to transport it. A small dog can be carried by one person simply by grasping the loose skin at the nape of the neck with one hand and placing the other hand under the dog's hips.

Burns from chemicals should first be treated by flushing the coat with plain water, taking care to protect the dog's eyes and ears. A baking soda solution can then be applied to neutralize the chemical further. If the burned area is small, a bland ointment should be applied. If the burned area is large, more extensive treatment will be required, as well as veterinary care.

Burns from hot liquid or hot metals should be treated by applying a bland ointment, provided the burned area is small. Burns over large areas should be treated by a veterinarian.

Electric shock usually results because an owner negligently leaves an electric cord exposed where the dog can chew on it. If possible, disconnect the cord before touching the dog. Otherwise, yank the cord from the dog's mouth so you will not receive a shock when you try to help him. If the dog is unconscious, artificial respiration and stimulants will be required, so a veterinarian should be consulted at once.

Fractures require immediate professional attention. A broken bone should be immobilized while the dog is transported to the veterinarian but no attempt should be made to splint it.

Poisoning is more often accidental than deliberate, but whichever the case, symptoms and treatment are the same. If the poisoning is not discovered immediately, the dog may be found unconscious. His mouth will be slimy, he will tremble, have difficulty breathing, and possibly go into convulsions. Veterinary treatment must be secured immediately.

If you find the dog eating something you know to be poisonous, induce vomiting immediately by repeatedly forcing the dog to swallow a mixture of equal parts of hydrogen peroxide and water. Delay of even a few minutes may result in death. When the contents of the stomach have been emptied, force the dog to swallow raw egg white, which will slow absorption of the poison. Then call the veterinarian. Provide him with information as to the type of poison, and follow his advice as to further treatment.

Some chemicals are toxic even though not swallowed, so before using a product, make sure it can be used safely around pets.

Severe bleeding from a leg can be controlled by applying a tourniquet between the wound and the body, but the tourniquet must be loosened at ten-minute intervals. Severe bleeding from head or body can be controlled by placing a cloth or gauze pad over the wound, then applying firm pressure with the hand.

To treat minor cuts, first trim the hair from around the wound, then wash the area with warm soapy water and apply a mild antiseptic such as tincture of metaphen.

Shock is usually the aftermath of severe injury and requires immediate veterinary attention. The dog appears dazed, lips and tongue are pale, and breathing is shallow. The dog should be wrapped in blankets and kept warm, and if possible, kept lying down with his head lower than his body.

Bacterial and Viral Diseases

Distemper takes many and varied forms, so it is sometimes difficult for even experienced veterinarians to diagnose. It is the number one killer of dogs, and although it is not unknown in older dogs, its victims are usually puppies. While some dogs do recover, permanent damage to the brain or nervous system is often sustained. Symptoms may include lethargy, diarrhea, vomiting, reduced appetite, cough, nasal discharge, inflammation of the eyes, and a rise in temperature. If distemper is suspected, a veterinarian must be consulted at once, for early treatment is essential. Effective preventive measures lie in inoculation. Shots for temporary immunity should be given all puppies within a few weeks after whelping, and the permanent inoculations should be given as soon thereafter as possible.

Hardpad has been fairly prevalent in Great Britain for a number of years, and its incidence in the United States is increasing. Symptoms are similar to those of distemper, but as the disease progresses, the pads of the feet harden and eventually peel. Chances of recovery are not favorable unless prompt veterinary care is secured.

Infectious hepatitis in dogs affects the liver, as does the human form, but apparently is not transmissible to man. Symptoms are similar to those of distemper, and the disease rapidly reaches the acute state. Since hepatitis is often fatal, prompt veterinary treatment is essential. Effective vaccines are available and should be provided all puppies. A combination distemper-hepatitis vaccine is sometimes used.

Leptospirosis is caused by a micro-organism often transmitted by contact with rats, or by ingestion of food contaminated by rats. The disease can be transmitted to man, so anyone caring for an afflicted dog must take steps to avoid infection. Symptoms include vomiting, loss of appetite, diarrhea, fever, depression and lethargy, redness of eyes and gums, and sometimes jaundice. Since permanent kidney damage may result, veterinary treatment should be secured immediately.

Rabies is a disease that is always fatal—and it is transmissible to man. It is caused by a virus that attacks the nervous system and is present in the saliva of an infected animal. When an infected animal bites another, the virus is transmitted to the new victim. It may also enter the body through cuts and scratches that come in contact with saliva containing the virus.

All warm-blooded animals are subject to rabies and it may be transmitted by foxes, skunks, squirrels, horses, and cattle as well as dogs. Anyone bitten by a dog (or other animal) should see his physician immediately, and health and law enforcement officials should be notified. Also, if your dog is bitten by another animal, consult your veterinarian immediately.

In most areas, rabies shots are required by law. Even if not required, all dogs should be given anti-rabies vaccine, for it is an effective preventive measure.

Dietary Deficiency Diseases

Rickets afflicts puppies not provided sufficient calcium and Vitamin D. Symptoms include lameness, arching of neck and back, and a tendency of the legs to bow. Treatment consists of providing adequate amounts of dicalcium phosphate and Vitamin D and exposing the dog to sunlight. If detected and treated before reaching an advanced stage, bone damage may be lessened somewhat, although it cannot be corrected completely.

Osteomalacia, similar to rickets, may occur in adult dogs. Treatment is the same as for rickets, but here, too, prevention is preferable to cure. Permanent deformities resulting from rickets or osteomalacia will not be inherited, so once victims recover, they can be used for breeding.

External Parasites

Fleas, lice, mites, and ticks can be eradicated in the dog's quarters by regular use of one of the insecticide sprays with a four to six weeks' residual effect. Bedding, blankets, and pillows should be laundered frequently and treated with an insecticide. Treatment for external parasites varies, depending upon the parasite involved, but a number of good dips and powders are available.

Fleas may be eliminated by dusting the coat thoroughly with flea powder at frequent intervals during the summer months when fleas are a problem.

Flea collars are very effective in keeping a dog free of fleas. However, some animals are allergic to the chemicals in the collars, so caution must be observed when the collar is used and the skin of the neck area must be checked frequently and the collar removed if the skin becomes irritated. Care must also be taken that the collar is not fastened too tightly, and any excess at the end must be cut off to prevent the dog from chewing it. The collar should be removed if it becomes wet (or even damp) and should always be removed before the dog is bathed and not replaced around the dog's neck again until the coat is completely dry. For a dog which reacts to the flea collar, a medallion to be hung from the regular collar is available. This will eliminate direct skin contact and thus any allergic reaction will be avoided. The medallion should, of course, be removed when the dog is bathed.

Lice may be eradicated by applying dips formulated especially for this purpose to the dog's coat. A fine-toothed comb should

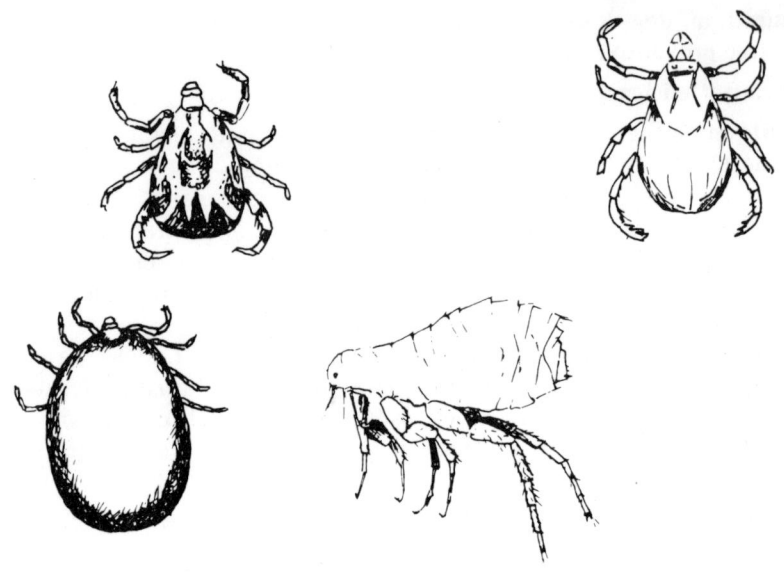

Common external parasites. Above, American dog ticks—left, female and right, male (much enlarged). Lower left, female tick, engorged. Lower right, dog flea (much enlarged).

then be used to remove dead lice and eggs, which are firmly attached to the coat.

Mites live deep in the ear canal, producing irritation to the lining of the ear and causing a brownish-black, dry type discharge. Plain mineral oil or ear ointment should be swabbed on the inner surface of the ear twice a week until mites are eliminated.

Ticks may carry Rocky Mountain spotted fever, so, to avoid possible infection, they should be removed from the dog only with tweezers and should be destroyed by burning (or by dropping them into insecticide). Heavy infestation can be controlled by sponging the coat daily with a solution containing a special tick dip.

Among other preparations available for controlling parasites on the dog's body are some that can be given internally. Since dosage must be carefully controlled, these preparations should not be used without consulting a veterinarian.

Internal Parasites

Internal parasites, with the exception of the tapeworm, may be transmitted from a mother dog to the puppies. Infestation may also result from contact with infected bedding or through access to a yard where an infected dog relieves himself. The types that may infest dogs are roundworms, whipworms, tapeworms, hookworms, and heartworms. All cause similar symptoms: a generally unthrifty appearance, stary coat, dull eyes, weakness and emaciation despite a ravenous appetite, coughing, vomiting, diarrhea, and sometimes bloody stools. Not all symptoms are present in every case, of course.

A heavy infestation with any type of worm is a serious matter and treatment must be started early and continued until the dog is free of the parasite or the dog's health will suffer seriously. Death may even result.

Promiscuous dosing for worms is dangerous and different types of worms require different treatment. So if you suspect your dog has worms, ask your veterinarian to make a microscopic examination of the feces, and to prescribe appropriate treatment if evidence of worm infestation is found.

LIFE CYCLE OF THE HEARTWORM

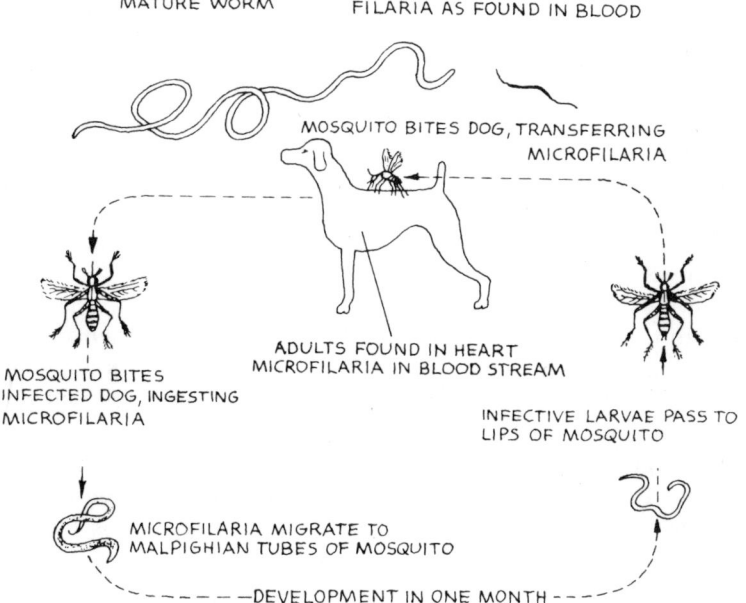

Heartworms were once thought to be a problem confined to the Southern part of the United States but they have become an increasingly common problem in Middle Western States. The larva is transmitted from dog to dog through the bite of the mosquito, and eight to nine months may elapse from the time the dog is bitten until the heartworm is mature. Once they have entered the bloodstream, heartworms mature in the heart, where they interfere with heart action. Symptoms include lethargy, chronic coughing, and loss of weight. Having the dog's blood examined microscopically is the only way the tiny larvae (called microfilaria) can be detected. Eradication of heartworms is extremely difficult, so a veterinarian well versed in this field should be consulted. In an area where mosquitoes are prevalent, it is well to protect the dog by keeping him in a screened-in area.

Hookworms are found in puppies as well as adult dogs. When excreted in the feces, the mature worm looks like a thread and is about three-quarters of an inch in length. Eradication is a serious problem in areas where the soil is infested with the worms, for the dog may then become reinfested after treatment. Consequently, medication usually must be repeated at intervals, and the premises—including the grounds where the dog exercises—must be treated and must be kept well drained. You may wish to consult your veterinarian regarding the vaccine for the prevention of hookworms in dogs which was licensed recently by the United States Department of Agriculture.

Roundworms are the most common of all the worms that may infest the dog, for most puppies are born with them or become infested with them shortly after birth. Roundworms vary in length from two to eight inches and can be detected readily through microscopic examination of the feces. At maturity, upon excretion, the roundworm will spiral into a circle, but after it dies it resembles a cut rubber band.

If you suspect that a puppy may have roundworms, check its gums and tongue. If the puppy is heavily infested, the worms will cause anemia and the gums and the tongue will be a very pale pink color. If the puppy is anemic, the veterinarian probably will prescribe a tonic in addition to the proper worm medicine.

Tapeworms require an intermediate host, usually the flea or the louse, but they sometimes are found in raw fish, so a dog can become infested by swallowing a flea or a louse, or by eating infested fish.

LIFE CYCLE OF THE HOOKWORM

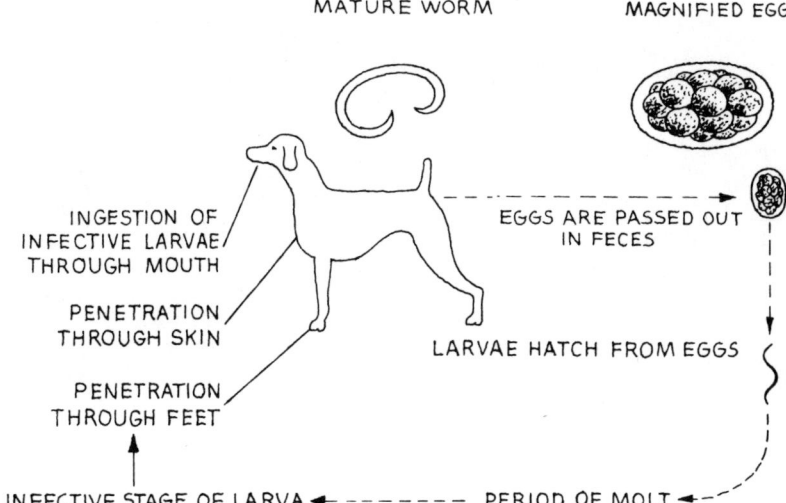

LIFE CYCLE OF THE COMMON ROUNDWORM

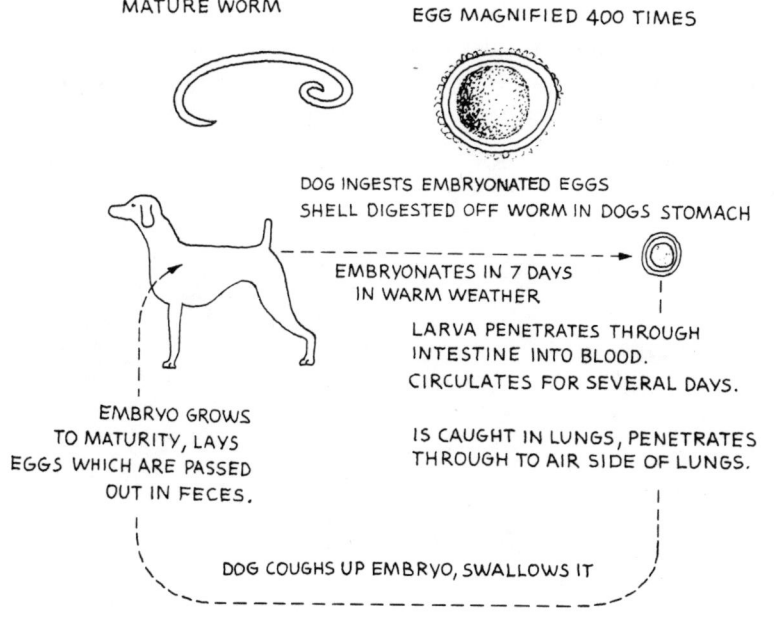

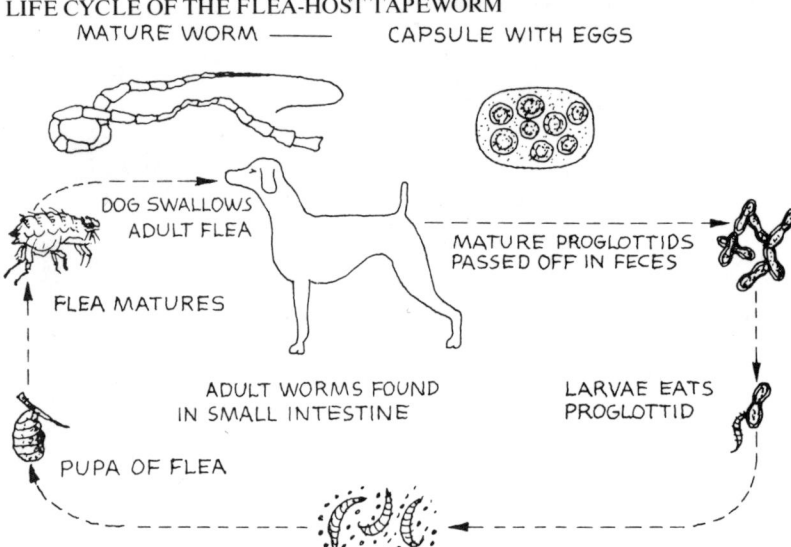

LIFE CYCLE OF THE FLEA-HOST TAPEWORM

A complete tapeworm can be two to three feet long. The head and neck of the tapeworm are small and threadlike, while the body is made up of segments like links of a sausage, which are about half an inch long and flat. Segments of the body separate from the worm and will be found in the feces or will hang from the coat around the anus and when dry will resemble dark grains of rice.

The head of the tapeworm is imbedded in the lining of the intestine where the worm feeds on the blood of the dog. The difficulty

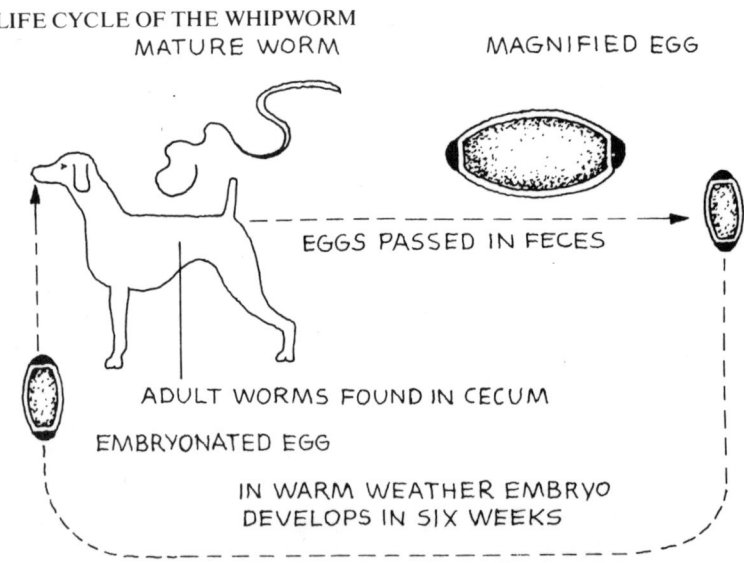

LIFE CYCLE OF THE WHIPWORM

in eradicating the tapeworm lies in the fact that most medicines have a laxative action which is too severe and which pulls the body from the head so the body is eliminated with the feces, but the implanted head remains to start growing a new body. An effective medication is a tablet which does not dissolve until it reaches the intestine where it anesthetizes the worm to loosen the head before expulsion.

Whipworms are more common in the eastern states than in states along the West Coast, but whipworms may infest dogs in any section of the United States. Whipworms vary in length from two to four inches and are tapered in shape so they resemble a buggy whip—which accounts for the name.

At maturity, the whipworm migrates into the caecum, where it is difficult to reach with medication. A fecal examination will show whether whipworms are present, so after treatment, it is best to have several examinations made in order to be sure the dog is free of them.

Skin Problems

Skin problems usually cause persistent itching. However, **follicular mange** does not usually do so but is evidenced by moth-eaten-looking patches, especially about the head and along the back. **Sarcoptic mange** produces severe itching and is evidenced by patchy, crusty areas on body, legs, and abdomen. Any evidence suggesting either should be called to the attention of a veterinarian. Both require extensive treatment and both may be contracted by humans.

Allergies are not readily distinguished from other skin troubles except through laboratory tests. However, dog owners should be alert to the fact that various coat dressings and shampoos, or simply bathing the dog too often, may produce allergic skin reactions.

Eczema is characterized by extreme itching, redness of the skin and exudation of serous matter. It may result from a variety of causes, and the exact cause in a particular case may be difficult to determine. Relief may be secured by dusting the dog twice a week with a soothing powder containing a fungicide and an insecticide.

Other Health Problems

Clogged anal glands cause intense discomfort, which the dog may attempt to relieve by scooting himself along the floor on his haunches. These glands, located on either side of the anus, se-

crete a substance that enables the dog to expel the contents of the rectum. If they become clogged, they may give the dog an unpleasant odor and when neglected, serious infection may result. Contents of the glands can be easily expelled into a wad of cotton, which should be held under the tail with the left hand. Then, using the right hand, pressure should be exerted with the thumb on one side of the anus, the forefinger on the other. The normal secretion is brownish in color, with an unpleasant odor. The presence of blood or pus indicates infection and should be called to the attention of a veterinarian.

Eye problems of a minor nature—redness or occasional discharge—may be treated with a few drops of boric acid solution (2%) or salt solution (1 teaspoonful table salt to 1 pint sterile water). Cuts on the eyeball, bruises close to the eyes, or persistent discharge should be treated only by a veterinarian.

Heat exhaustion is a serious (and often fatal) problem caused by exposure to extreme heat. Usually it occurs when a thoughtless owner leaves the dog in a closed vehicle without proper shade and ventilation. Even on a day when outside temperatures do not seem excessively high, heat builds up rapidly to an extremely high temperature in a closed vehicle parked in direct sunlight or even in partial shade. Many dogs and young children die each year from being left in an inadequately ventilated vehicle. To prevent such a tragedy, an owner or parent should never leave a dog or child unattended in a vehicle even for a short time.

During hot weather, whenever a dog is taken for a ride in an air-conditioned automobile, the cool air should be reduced gradually when nearing the destination, for the sudden shock of going from cool air to extremely hot temperatures can also result in shock and heat exhaustion.

Symptoms of heat exhaustion include rapid and difficult breathing and near or complete collapse. After removing the victim from the vehicle, first aid treatment consists of sponging cool water over the body to reduce temperature as quickly as possible. Immediate medical treatment is essential in severe cases of heat exhaustion.

Care of the Ailing or Injured Dog

A dog that is seriously ill, requiring surgical treatment, transfusions, or intravenous feeding, must be hospitalized. One requiring less complicated treatment is better cared for at home, but it is essential that the dog be kept in a quiet environment. Preferably his bed should be in a room apart from family activity, yet close at hand, so his condition can be checked frequently. Clean bedding and adequate warmth are essential, as are a constant supply of fresh, cool water, and foods to tempt the appetite.

Special equipment is not ordinarily needed, but the following items will be useful in caring for a sick dog, as well as in giving first aid for injuries:

petroleum jelly	tincture of metaphen
rubbing alcohol	cotton, gauze, and adhesive tape
mineral oil	burn ointment
rectal thermometer	tweezers
hydrogen peroxide	boric acid solution (2%)

If special medication is prescribed, it may be administered in any one of several ways. A pill or small capsule may be concealed in a small piece of meat, which the dog will usually swallow with no problem. A large capsule may be given by holding the dog's mouth open, inserting the capsule as far as possible down the throat, then holding the mouth closed until the dog swallows. Liquid medicine should be measured into a small bottle or test tube. Then, if the corner of the dog's lip is pulled out while the head is tilted upward, the liquid can be poured between the lips and teeth, a small amount at a time. If he refuses to swallow, keeping the dog's head tilted and stroking his throat will usually induce swallowing.

Liquid medication may also be given by use of a hypodermic syringe without a needle. The syringe is slipped into the side of the mouth and over the rise at the back of the tongue, and the medicine is "injected" slowly down the throat. This is especially good for medicine with a bad taste, for the medicine does not touch the taste buds in the front part of the tongue. It also eliminates spills and guarantees that all the medicine goes in.

Foods offered the sick dog should be particularly nutritious and easily digested. Meals should be smaller than usual and offered at more frequent intervals. If the dog is reluctant to eat, offer food he particularly likes and warm it slightly to increase aroma and thus make it more tempting.

The Stone-Age Dog.

A Spotted Dog from India, "Parent of the modern Coach Dog."

History of the Genus Canis

The history of man's association with the dog is a fascinating one, extending into the past at least seventy centuries, and involving the entire history of civilized man from the early Stone Age to the present.

The dog, technically a member of the genus *Canis*, belongs to the zoological family group *Canidae*, which also includes such animals as wolves, foxes, jackals, and coyotes. In the past it was generally agreed that the dog resulted from the crossing of various members of the family *Canidae*. Recent findings have amended this theory somewhat, and most authorities now feel the jackal probably has no direct relationship with the dog. Some believe dogs are descended from wolves and foxes, with the wolf the main progenitor. As evidence, they cite the fact that the teeth of the wolf are identical in every detail with those of the dog, whereas the teeth of the jackal are totally different.

Still other authorities insist that the dog always has existed as a separate and distinct animal. This group admits that it is possible for a dog to mate with a fox, coyote, or wolf, but points out that the resulting puppies are unable to breed with each other, although they can breed with stock of the same genus as either parent. Therefore, they insist, it was impossible for a new and distinct genus to have developed from such crossings. They then cite the fact that any dog can be mated with any other dog and the progeny bred among themselves. These researchers point out, too, heritable characteristics that are different in these animals. For instance, the pupil of the eye of the fox is eliptical and vertical, while the pupil is round in the dog, wolf, and coyote. Tails, too, differ considerably, for tails of foxes, coyotes, and wolves always drop behind them, while those of dogs may be carried over the back or straight up.

Much conjecture centers on two wild dog species that still exist—the Dingo of Australia, and the Dhole in India. Similar in appearance, both are reddish in color, both have rather long, slender jaws, both have rounded ears that stand straight up, and both species hunt in packs. Evidence indicates that they had the same ancestors. Yet, today, they live in areas that are more than 4,000 miles apart.

Despite the fact that it is impossible to determine just when the dog first appeared as a distinct species, archeologists have found definite proof that the dog was the first animal domesticated by man. When man lived by tracking, trapping, and killing game, the dog added to the forces through which man discovered and captured the quarry. Man shared his primitive living quarters with the dog, and the two together devoured the prey. Thus, each helped to sustain the life of the other. The dog assisted man, too, by defending the campsite against marauders. As man gradually became civilized, the dog's usefulness was extended to guarding the other animals man domesticated, and, even before the wheel was invented, the dog served as a beast of burden. In fact, archeological findings show that aboriginal peoples of Switzerland and Ireland used the dog for such purposes long before they learned to till the soil.

Cave drawings from the palaeolithic era, which was the earliest part of the Old World Stone Age, include hunting scenes in which a rough, canine-like form is shown alongside huntsmen. One of these drawings is believed to be 50,000 years old, and gives credence to the theory that all dogs are descended from a primitive type ancestor that was neither fox nor wolf.

Archeological findings show that Europeans of the New Stone Age possessed a breed of dogs of wolf-like appearance, and a similar breed has been traced through the successive Bronze Age and Iron Age. Accurate details are not available, though, as to the external appearance of domesticated dogs prior to historic times (roughly four to five thousand years ago).

Early records in Chaldean and Egyptian tombs show that several distinct and well-established dog types had been developed by about 3700 B.C. Similar records show that the early people of the Nile Valley regarded the dog as a god, often burying it as a mummy in special cemeteries and mourning its death.

Some of the early Egyptian dogs had been given names, such as Akna, Tarn, and Abu, and slender dogs of the Greyhound type and a short-legged Terrier type are depicted in drawings found in Egyptian royal tombs that are at least 5,000 years old. The Afghan Hound and the Saluki are shown in drawings of only slightly later times. Another type of ancient Egyptian dog was much heavier and more powerful, with short coat and massive head. These

Bas-relief of Hunters with Nets and Mastiffs. From the walls of Assurbanipal's palace at Nineveh 668-626 B.C. *British Museum.*

probably hunted by scent, as did still another type of Egyptian dog that had a thick furry coat, a tail curled almost flat over the back, and erect "prick" ears.

Early Romans and Greeks mentioned their dogs often in literature, and both made distinctions between those that hunted by sight and those that hunted by scent. The Romans' canine classifications were similar to those we use now. In addition to dogs comparable to the Greek sight and scent hounds, the ancient Romans had Canes *villatici* (housedogs) and Canes *pastorales* (sheepdogs), corresponding to our present-day working dogs.

The dog is mentioned many times in the Old Testament. The first reference, in Genesis, leads some Biblical scholars to assert that man and dog have been companions from the time man was created. And later Biblical references bring an awareness of the diversity in breeds and types existing thousands of years ago.

As civilization advanced, man found new uses for dogs. Some required great size and strength. Others needed less of these characteristics but greater agility and better sight. Still others needed an accentuated sense of smell. As time went on, men kept those puppies that suited specific purposes especially well and bred them together. Through ensuing generations of selective breeding, desirable characteristics appeared with increasing frequency. Dogs used in a particular region for a special purpose gradually became more like each other, yet less like dogs of other areas used for different purposes. Thus were established the foundations for the various breeds we have today.

The American Kennel Club, the leading dog organization in the United States, divides the various breeds into six "Groups," based on similarity of purposes for which they were developed.

"Sporting Dogs" include the Pointers, Setters, Spaniels, and Retrievers that were developed by sportsmen interested in hunting game birds. Most of the Pointers and Setters are of comparatively recent origin. Their development parallels the development of sporting firearms, and most of them evolved in the British Isles. Exceptions are the Weimaraner, which was developed in Germany, and the Vizsla, or Hungarian Pointer, believed to have been developed by the Magyar hordes that swarmed over Central Europe a

Bas-relief of Assyrian Mastiffs hunting wild horses. *British Museum.*

thousand years ago. The Irish were among the first to use Spaniels, though the name indicates that the original stock may have come from Spain. Two Sporting breeds, the American Water Spaniel and the Chesapeake Bay Retriever, were developed entirely in the United States.

"Hounds," among which are Dachshunds, Beagles, Bassets, Harriers, and Foxhounds, are used singly, in pairs, or in packs to "course" (or run) and hunt for rabbits, foxes, and various rodents. But little larger, the Norwegian Elkhound is used in its native country to hunt big game—moose, bear, and deer.

The smaller Hound breeds hunt by scent, while the Irish Wolfhound, Borzoi, Scottish Deerhound, Saluki, and Greyhound hunt by sight. The Whippet, Saluki, and Greyhound are notably fleet of foot, and racing these breeds (particularly the Greyhound) is popular sport.

The Bloodhound is a member of the Hound Group that is known world-wide for its scenting ability. On the other hand, the Basenji is a comparatively rare Hound breed and has the distinction of being the only dog that cannot bark.

"Working Dogs" have the greatest utilitarian value of all modern dogs and contribute to man's welfare in diverse ways. The Boxer, Doberman Pinscher, Rottweiler, German Shepherd, Great Dane, and Giant Schnauzer are often trained to serve as sentries and aid police in patrolling streets. The German Shepherd is especially noted as a guide dog for the blind. The Collie, the various breeds of Sheepdogs, and the two Corgi breeds are known throughout the world for their extraordinary herding ability. And the exploits of the St. Bernard and Newfoundland are legendary, their records for saving lives unsurpassed.

The Siberian Husky, the Samoyed, and the Alaskan Malamute are noted for tremendous strength and stamina. Had it not been for these hardy Northern breeds, the great polar expeditions might never have taken place, for Admiral Byrd used these dogs to reach points inaccessible by other means. Even today, with our jet-age transportation, the Northern breeds provide a more practical means of travel in frigid areas than do modern machines.

"Terriers" derive their name from the Latin *terra,* meaning "earth," for all of the breeds in this Group are fond of burrowing. Terriers hunt by digging into the earth to rout rodents and fur-bearing animals such as badgers, woodchucks, and otters. Some breeds are expected merely to force the animals from their dens in

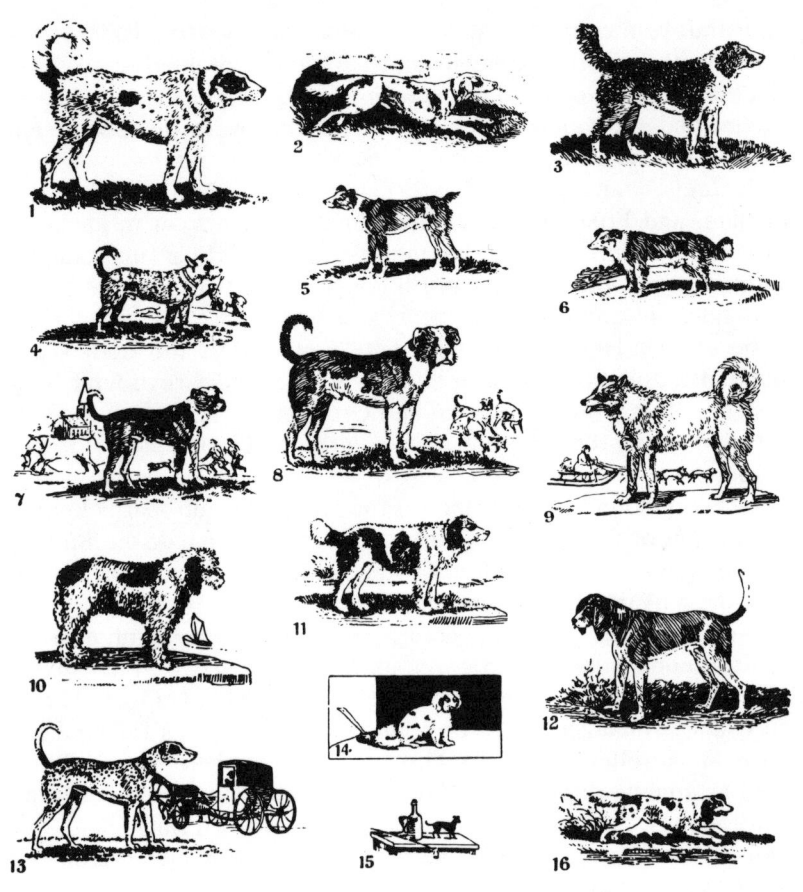

1. The Newfoundland. 2. The English Setter. 3. The Large Water-spaniel. 4. The Terrier. 5. The Cur-dog. 6. The Shepherd's Dog. 7. The Bulldog. 8. The Mastiff. 9. The Greenland Dog. 10. The Rough Water-dog. 11. The Small Water-spaniel. 12. The Old English Hound. 13. The Dalmatian or Coach-dog. 14. The Comporter (very much of a Papillon). 15. "Toy Dog, Bottle, Glass, and Pipe." *From a vignette.* 16. The Springer or Cocker. *From Thomas Bewick's "General History of Quadrupeds" (1790).*

order that the hunter can complete the capture. Others are expected to find and destroy the prey, either on the surface or under the ground.

Terriers come in a wide variety of sizes, ranging from such large breeds as the Airedale and Kerry Blue to such small ones as the Skye, the Dandie Dinmont, the West Highland White, and the Scottish Terrier. England, Ireland, and Scotland produced most of the Terrier breeds, although the Miniature Schnauzer was developed in Germany.

"Toys," as the term indicates, are small breeds. Although they make little claim to usefulness other than as ideal housepets, Toy dogs develop as much protective instinct as do larger breeds and serve effectively in warning of the approach of strangers.

Origins of the Toys are varied. The Pekingese was developed as the royal dog of China more than two thousand years before the birth of Christ. The Chihuahua, smallest of the Toys, originated in Mexico and is believed to be a descendant of the Techichi, a dog of great religious significance to the Aztecs, while the Italian Greyhound was popular in the days of ancient Pompeii.

"Non-Sporting Dogs" include a number of popular breeds of varying ancestry. The Standard and Miniature Poodles were developed in France for the purpose of retrieving game from water. The Bulldog originated in Great Britain and was bred for the purpose of "baiting" bulls. The Chow Chow apparently originated centuries ago in China, for it is pictured in a bas relief dated to the Han dynasty of about 150 B.C.

The Dalmatian served as a carriage dog in Dalmatia, protecting travelers in bandit-infested regions. The Keeshond, recognized as the national dog of Holland, is believed to have originated in the Arctic or possibly the Sub-Arctic. The Schipperke, sometimes erroneously described as a Dutch dog, originated in the Flemish provinces of Belgium. And the Lhasa Apso came from Tibet, where it is known as "Abso Seng Kye," the "Bark Lion Sentinel Dog."

During the thousands of years that man and dog have been closely associated, a strong affinity has been built up between the two. The dog has more than earned his way as a helper, and his faithful, selfless devotion to man is legendary. The ways in which the dog has proved his intelligence, his courage, and his dependability in situations of stress are amply recorded in the countless tales of canine heroism that highlight the pages of history, both past and present.

Dogs in Woodcuts. (*1st row*) (LEFT) "Maltese dog with shorter hair"; (RIGHT) "Spotted sporting dog trained to catch game"; (*2nd row*) (LEFT) Sporting white dog; (RIGHT) "Spanish dog with floppy ears": (*3rd row*) (LEFT) "French dog"; (RIGHT) "Mad dog of Grevinus"; (*4th row*) (LEFT) Hairy Maltese dog; (RIGHT) "English fighting dog ... of horrid aspect." *From Aldrovandus (1637).*

Early History of the Old English Sheepdog

The new breed enthusiast, eagerly reading all the available books and articles written about the Old English Sheepdog, is disappointed to learn that the origin of the Bobtail cannot now be determined. Even worse, the farther back in time he goes in his search for information on the breed in the earlier books, the more confused he becomes.

The Old English Sheepdog is considered to be one of the oldest breeds of dog we have, yet in most of the books written before this century, among the descriptions of the several sorts of Sheepdogs and Collies there seldom seems to have been any unmistakable description of our breed as a distinct one. In some cases, only the fact that a variety of the "Collie" or "Colly" is described as being long-haired and without a tail leads one to conclude that the dog described may, in fact, have been our friend.

One reason for the absence of a reliable record stems from the fact that in ancient times few breeds except those reserved by the nobility for their hunting were thought worthy of special notice. Some of the earliest records, in fact, lump the common farm dogs together simply as "bandogs," "mastiffs," or (in Wales) "Curs."

However, if one considers what the circumstances of those early days must have been in the world of dogs, it is less surprising that confusion occurred. What with the slower communications, the greater isolation of communities, and the lack of any kennel clubs to differentiate the breeds and encourage selective breeding, one can readily imagine the difficulty of describing any distinct type of dog on the basis of what must have been, in many respects, an author's limited observation.

Imagine a few generations of non-selective crossbreeding today among all of the various British Collies and Sheepdogs, with perhaps a little of this and that from other breeds thrown in occasionally, and I suppose the results might approximate the descriptions given for the shepherds' and drovers' dogs in most of the early books. Rather mixed and inconsistent, certainly. The confusion is compounded by the fact that the misconceptions of one author were apparently taken up and repeated by the next with conviction and finality. The books make fascinating reading, but cannot be interpreted as conforming in more than the broadest sense to the modern concepts of the breeds.

When their descriptions can be passably sorted out, we find that the early writers treated the Old English Sheepdog as being indigenous to the British Isles and developing somewhat differently in the different areas. It seems certain that the breed has been known there, if by different names in different times and areas, for at least two hundred years. Not until the latter part of the nineteenth century, however, did any significant number of fanciers attempt to breed selectively a single identifiable type of "Old English Sheepdog." I think it is generally considered, however, that the dogs of today descended primarily from stock originating in the Downs of Sussex and perhaps other nearby areas in southern England.

So we are left with the only authoritative record of the breed beginning with the founding of the English breed club and its adoption of the Standard (unchanged there today) in 1888; and even after that, it remained for the breeders to eliminate the brown color that a number of the breed carried up to that time. Only the systematic registration of purebred dogs and the advent of photography have eliminated some of the pitfalls of personal recollection and relieved us of some of the speculation and conjecture which, repeated often enough, tend to take on the aura of gospel.

Among British writers before 1900, the Old English Sheepdog (or a bob-tailed dog fitting his general description) has been variously termed:

The Sussex or Old English Sheepdog (1811)
British Drover's Dog (1845)
Scotch Colly (1846)
The Drover's Dog (1853)

Old picture postcard which carries the notation "Miss I. Webster, Pastelblue." No date is shown on the card.

English Sheep-dog (1861)
Sheepdog (Short-tailed English) (1879 *Stud Book*)
English Short-tailed Colley (1881 *Stud Book*)
Scotch Bob-tailed Sheepdog (1881)
The Bob-Tailed Sheepdog (1882)
Cur (in the old English sense, possibly from "curtail" or "curtal," the latter being an old word meaning "to dock") (1888)
Drover's Bob-tailed Collie [1895 (?)]
Cotswold Sheepdog (?)
Smithfield Sheepdog (there is some dispute on this as being a purebred OES)

Among writers in this century, speculation has abounded concerning the origin of the Old English Sheepdog, and there seems to have been no supported basis for any of it except the casting about among similar sorts of dogs the world over for a type that could conceivably have been the progenitor of the breed. One of the several speculations, repeated so often that it has almost become myth, is that the original Old English Sheepdog could have developed from a cross between the Russian Owtchar (variously spelled) and the Scotch Bearded Collie, which it certainly resembles in several respects.

Why the tail docking? We do not know for sure why the Old English Sheepdog has traditionally had his tail docked. Several highly-respected breeders writing on the breed have insisted that occasionally some of them are born without tails, an anomaly that early writers attributed to generations of docking; but of course scientists today are unanimous in holding that such a genetic alteration is impossible.

Several different reasons for the custom have been suggested. The first, and probably the most likely one (if majority opinion is persuasive), is that by law in the old days in Britain, working dogs were not subject to tax, and that a docked tail was the accepted proof that a dog was a working dog. (One might well ask, then, why were not *all* working dogs so treated?)

Another old theory was that in the days when royalty and nobility held hunting preserves, no common man was permitted to keep a dog that could hunt game. It was believed that without a tail, the dog was rudderless and poorly adapted to the quick turns required for the chase, and so the common man could keep a dog only if its tail had been docked. Others, by somewhat similar reasoning, hold that the docking was intended to discourage the dog from being distracted by game and giving chase when he was at work.

A theory found in only the very oldest records and often repeated, though it is based only on ancient superstition, was that a docked dog would never go mad. I find only one mention of three other speculations about the justification for docking the tail: one, that it strengthens the dog's back; another, that it increases the dog's speed (hardly consistent with the theory of hindering a chase); and a third, that without a tail the dog must circle the flock widely rather than go straight at it and possibly scatter it.

Why the wall-eyed dog? The wall-eyed dog, according to some reports, was especially valued by shepherds because of a superstition that at night the one blue eye could better distinguish wolves from the flock and see evil spirits. The latter, at least, is a skill not attributed to the brown-eyed dog. Another possibly widely-held (but equally unfounded) belief was that such a dog would never go blind.

I am indebted to Lawrence E. Jones of Champaign, Illinois, for some of the following dates and milestones in the history of the evolution of the Old English Sheepdog:

600 B.C. to 200 A.D.—Herdsmen's dogs of the large, powerful, heavy-coated variety brought to Britain with the Celtic invaders (600-75 B.C.) and/or during the Roman invasions (beginning 55 B.C.). Sole function to protect shepherds and flocks.

1400 to c. 1600—Several accounts of sheepdogs with docked tails. In *King Lear* (1605), Shakespeare mentions (among others) a " . . . bobtail tike . . . " (Act V, Sc. vi, line 73.) Modern authority gives "tike" the definition of "cur" or "dog" but in Shakespeare's day the term "cur" would not have the modern connotation of mongrel, since purebred dogs did not exist as such then.

1771—John Boydell's engraving of a painting by Gainsborough shows the Duke of Buccleuh with his arms clasped about a dog now considered by many to have been an Old English Sheepdog. It is seated and there is no view of the dog's rear and it seems to be too small for our modern conception of the OES. Characteristic of the OES, however, the dog has its right paw laid gracefully across the Duke's wrist.

1803—*Sportsman's Cabinet,* a standard reference book on dogs, published an engraving by J. Scott of a painting by Philip Reinagle supposed by modern fanciers to be an illustration of the OES. Some see the dog as representing a more northern variety, possibly more closely resembling the Bearded Collie. The dog pictured has a medium-length tail well covered with coat. The accompanying article by "Taplin" describes a "Scotch Collie."

A Bob-Tailed Sheep Dog. From the painting by Cooper, 1835.

Henry, Third Duke of Buccleugh. John Boydell's engraving of a painting by Gainsborough, 1771.

1835—Painting by Sidney Cooper of an OES at rest, dated and titled by the artist, "From Nature." Probably the earliest known representation of the breed that is unquestionably representative of our concept of the breed today. Shepherds recalling the dogs of this period will later describe the OES, its usefulness for driving sheep and (especially) cattle to market, as well as for protecting flocks from predators and thieves. Act of Parliament bans "Blood Sports," ending bull-baiting and dog fight matches.

1840 to 1860—Several accounts suggesting several types of OES or differing types in various geographical areas: Youatt (1845), Richardson (1847), "Stonehenge" (J. H. Walsh) (1859 and subsequent editions—one, the fifth, as late as 1886), and Meyrick (1861). In 1905 Aubrey Hopwood, in the first book devoted exclusively to the OES, calls Stonehenge's description "everything that (the OES) should *not* be." In the fifth edition of his book, Stonehenge dismisses the Bob-Tailed Sheepdog with a single paragraph in which he says it is "without definite type." These are the several authors principally guilty of leaving us some confusing and contradictory descriptions of what the OES was, and one even ascribed to him a totally uncharacteristic temperament, though there is agreement among them that the breed is remarkably intelligent.

The Shepherd's Dog. (From *The Sportsman's Cabinet* 1803.) By P. Reinagle, R.A.

Old English Sheepdog Ch. Cupid's Dart. F. Wilmot, owner. A typical elastic gallop as seen by artist R. H. Moore. From *All About Dogs* by Charles Henry Lane, 1912.

A few of their misleading representations are perpetuated by some of the later writers.

About 1840—Mr. Edward Lloyd, Rhiwlas, Bala, Wales, imports OES from the South Downs of Sussex for breeding. His program, later continued by his son, Mr. R. J. Lloyd Price, is the first known attempt at serious breeding for type.

1859—First English dog show at Newcastle. Birmingham also has a show. "Sporting Dogs" only are exhibited. As yet there are no standards for judging.

1860-1861—"Other breeds" are added at shows. Leeds and Birmingham shows have "Shepherds Dog" classes, all varieties shown together. Manchester is added to the list of shows.

About 1860s—Dr. G. C. Edwardes-Ker, Woodbridge, Suffolk, begins a breeding program that will last more than thirty years and will produce a number of the great early OES. He was an early exporter of some of the first OES stock to reach America. He adopted a breeding program to eliminate the brown and brindle coats and to produce a larger dog. Not all fanciers agreed with his preference for the latter.

1863—Islington show has separate classes for "Scotch Sheepdogs" and "English Sheepdogs."

1873—OES have their first separate class at Curzon Hall, Birmingham. There are three entries, but Judge M. B. Wynn withholds first place. English Kennel Club ("The Kennel Club") founded.

1874—First volume of *The Kennel Club Stud Book* published.

1875—Continual rapid rise in OES entries begins. Dr. Edwardes-Ker's dogs are prominent among the winners.

1879—OES first appear in *The Kennel Club Stud Book,* Vol. V, under "Sheepdogs (Short-tailed English)."

1885—Dr. Edwardes-Ker and Freeman Lloyd write a breed Standard for OES.

1888—English "Old English Sheepdog Club" founded and Standard adopted. First President, Sir Humphrey de Trafford, holds office until 1911. Founders included Mr. William G. Weager, Dr. Edwardes-Ker, Mrs. Mayhew, Mr. J. Thomas, Mr. Freeman Lloyd, Mr. Parry Thomas. In 1905 Mr. Aubrey Hopwood will write of them, " . . . in those days there were about as many different types of bob-tails as there were members of the Club, and each member stood staunchly by his own." The OES entry at Curzon Hall, Birmingham, is twenty.

1889—Freeman Lloyd's pamphlet reprints his articles from an American publication, *Turf, Field, and Farm.* Mr. Lloyd's writings had considerable influence on the development of the breed in both England and America.

1894—First OESC Specialty Show. *The Collie or Sheepdog,* by Rawdon Lee, has a chapter devoted to the Bobtail, quoting Dr. Edwardes-Ker at length. The book accurately describes the correct type and uses the OES "Sir Cavendish" for illustration. That same year, Vero Shaw's book, *Illustrated Book of the Dog,* preserves the confusion of the earlier writers. He apparently considers the lack of a tail on the OES to be a "natural" condition, and he is probably most confused of all the writers in distinguishing between the Colly, Collie, and Scotch breeds.

1903/04—H. A. Tilley of the Tilley Brothers' Shepton Kennels comes to Westminster with entries, and on the second trip he helps found The Old English Sheepdog Club of America (ten members). (The OESCA is recognized by The American Kennel Club in 1905 and dates its existence from that time.) Crufts has eighty-four OES entries in 1904.

1905—Aubrey Hopwood publishes his *The Old English Sheepdog (From Puppyhood to Champion),* still rated as one of the best books on the breed. (It is reprinted in Wales in 1973 in a publication called *The Bobtail Directory.*)

1933—H. A. Tilley's book, *The Old English Sheepdog,* is privately printed. It is revised and enlarged in another private printing in 1937. He recalls his 1903 trip to the Westminster Show at Madison Square Garden in New York City. This is our best source of personal recollection about the best dogs around the beginning of this century.

Sheepdogs adapt to many ways of life, here as a side-car companion. Another, called "Alfie," tours Europe in a mobile camper with Owner-Author Peter Maas *(Serpico)*.

The Old English Sheepdog in the United States

In writing the history of the Old English Sheepdog in this country, one does so at the risk (and a great one it is!) of oversight and error resulting from the lack of authoritative source materials from the earliest days.

It may be helpful, first, to know something about canine registrations in this country. There were two important early canine registrations. One (later given to the AKC and incorporated as the beginning of their records) was by Dr. Nathaniel Rowe for the National American Kennel Club. He was the first President of the club which was organized in 1876 at Chicago. His first volume was published in 1879 (dogs registered in 1878) and it also included show records. Two additional volumes were published after another five years, and in 1887 The American Kennel Club, which had been organized in 1884, published the fourth volume when Dr. Rowe gave them his records. These constitute the beginning of the AKC's registrations.

In the meantime, there was another canine stud record, "The American Kennel Register," which was published monthly beginning in April 1883 and continuing for five volumes into 1887. It was compiled by Forest and Stream Publishing Company at New York City, but it is not a part of AKC official records. The magazine also reported early show results and may have been an important factor through its editorial comments in encouraging the organization of The American Kennel Club.

Another source of information (though possibly less authoritative than the first two) on early American shows is Arnold Burges' book, *The American Kennel and Sporting Field* (1876), which included an abbreviated history of the shows and a list of breeding records of sporting dogs. It must be noted that by and large, the early breeding records were those of sporting dogs which made up the major portion of show entries in those days.

It is pure conjecture, of course, but surely no one would be surprised to find that some OES types did reach our shores with immigrant families quite early in our history, though they had to have been working dogs whose owners never concerned themselves with breed lineage or dog shows.

For a number of years even after the OES was being shown and was firmly established as a registered breed in this country, the OES breed winners at the big and prestigious shows were mostly imports from England, and their owners were largely wealthy people on the east coast who could afford the luxury of professionally-staffed and well-stocked kennels and who imported the finest specimens to be found (and at very high prices), beginning especially in the first years of this century. It is to them, in fact, that we may be most indebted for the excellence of some of our American-bred dogs today; but not since 1938 has an imported OES taken Best-of-Breed at Westminster, though a Canadian dog did so in 1975, and went on to Best-in-Show.

There does apparently exist a record of the importation of an OES in 1844 (*American Agriculturist*, Vol. 3, 1844) by a B. Gates of Gap Grove in Lee County, Illinois, but there is no "official" record of an early OES immigrant until "Bob" was registered as No. 3163 in the January, 1886, *American Kennel Register* (not to be confused with AKC registrations). His date of birth has been given as February, 1885, and we are told that he was purchased that same year from M. H. Lowe of Wednesbury, England, by Glencoe (or Glencho) Kennels owned by Mr. S. M. Cleaver at East Bethlehem, Pennsylvania. A bitch, "Judith," was also imported by Mr. Cleaver. One source tells us she was whelped October 26, 1883, out of Dr. Edwardes-Ker's "Gipsy" in England and was sired by the same "Bob" already mentioned.

A litter whelped November 11, 1885, by Bob x Judith is the first known OES American-bred litter. The second recorded was that of breeder William Wade, Pittsburgh, Pennsylvania (Bob x Daisy). Bob was shown at Philadelphia on October 6, 1885, for the first OES win (Miscellaneous Class) in this country of which I have been able to find any mention.

"Dame Hester" from Bob and Judith's litter was shown at Milwaukee in 1886, which may be the first recorded entry of an American owner-bred OES in this country.

Dog shows in those early days were apparently often rather informal and haphazard affairs subject to no uniform rules or official breed standards. In one case, a show was reported cancelled because only one exhibitor showed up. The majority of entries were sporting dogs, and all varieties of Shepherd and Collie dogs might be mixed or shown in various Miscellaneous Classes. Sometimes

Loyalblu Feelin Groovy—eight weeks.

the Miscellaneous Classes included the most unbelievable freaks and "interesting" crossbreeds. Some order began to come out of chaos with the founding of The American Kennel Club in 1884, but as late as 1899, we are told, at the Specialty Show of the Collie Club of America it was Old English Sheepdogs which took the first three places in Open Dog and the fourth place in Open Bitch! In fairness, it must be admitted that the judge was an OES fancier.

In spite of these conditions, we have the record of another Glencoe import, "Sir Lucifer" (breeder: Dr. Edwardes-Ker by Sir Vanoc x Dame Margery, 1883), who won numerous Miscellaneous Classes throughout the country. At Westminster he was Second in 1886 and First in 1887 (Miscellaneous Classes), and is recorded on August 30, 1887, as being awarded a First in the "Bobtailed Sheepdog" Class at Hornellsville, New York, which may have been one of the earliest separate OES classes at American shows.

The first OES entry in the AKC registrations is "Gillie" (1898), a dog imported by J. Pierpont Morgan's Collie Kennel from Mr. Llewellyn (whelped September 1, 1896). He was a winner at shows here from 1899 to 1901. It may be noted that for a great number of years the dogs entered at shows did not have to be registered; they could be merely "listed" in the *Gazette* for a twenty-five cent fee (AKC Show Rules, March 1, 1898).

Anne Weisse with "Shaggy Boy" on a German mountaintop. No matter how big they get, many a Sheepdog continues to think of himself as a lapdog.

The first Old English Sheepdog AKC championships recorded were those in 1904 of Ch. Lady Stumpie and Ch. Potsford Bob. Both were imported dogs. The first was a bitch bred by Mr. Griffith-Lock (Major of Newport x Czarina, whelped June 30, 1896) and owned by Mr. and Mrs. William C. Eustis. The second was a dog (Lion x Judy, whelped in November, 1897) owned by Mrs. L. Trowbridge Martin.

Among the earliest OES American champions were four imported and owned by James A. Garland of New York and Rhode Island: Ch. Captain Rough Weather (1906), Ch. Dolly Gray (1906), Ch. King Edward (1907), and Ch. Ringlow's Sultan (1907). Probably the best known of the early champions was Ch. Stylish Boy (1906) (breeders: Potts and Shepherd, by Young Watch x Larkfield Watch Lass, whelped September 4, 1898, in England), who was owned by Mr. Reginald Vanderbilt. Three of Ch. Stylish Boy's sons were among the early champions: Ch. Kenvil Blinkers (1908) (breeder-owner: Mrs. H. W. Berryman by Ch. Stylish Boy x Kenvil Lady, whelped April 16, 1905), the first American-bred breeder-owned dog to become a champion; Ch. Rowsley Conquest (1906), owned by J. Scott McComb's Rowsley Kennels; and Mr. Vanderbilt's Ch. Sandy Point Rags.

Three of the other early champions were bred in England by the Tilley Brothers of Shepton fame: Ch. Crossroads Quality (1905), owned by Mrs. Richard Harding Davis; Ch. Gray Towers Peggy (1908), owned by W. W. Harrison; and Ch. Druid Content (1909), owned by Messrs. Wells and Hastings. In addition, the Tilleys had selected and exported seven others of the first fifteen AKC champions.

A 1914 publication lists the following additional OES Champions of Record: Ch. Dame Doris (1908), Ch. Slumber (1912), Ch. Midnight (1912), and Ch. Endcliffe Capricious, all owned by Mrs. Tyler Morse; Ch. Wenkroy's Rag(s) (1909) owned by H. L. Post; and Ch. Rumson Petticoat owned by Mrs. E. K. Clarke.

The first Canadian import to become an American champion was Mr. W. Welch Harrison's Ch. King Bob (breeder: W. S. Watts by Ch. King Edward x Sally Harkaway, whelped March 30, 1903), who finished in 1909.

Of course the percentage of imported dogs among those achieving championship status today is much smaller. In the five-year period from 1970 through 1974 inclusive there were 563 new OES champions, but only twenty-six of them were whelped abroad.

Typical OES pose. Register of Merit Dam, Greyfriar's Old Lace, Tamara Kennels.

Best-in-Show Ch. Sir Lancelot of Barvan, owned by Mr. and Mrs. Ronald Vanword, at the ninety-ninth annual dog show of the Westminster Kennel Club, February 10-11, 1975. Judge, Mr. Harry T. Peters, Jr. Handler, Malcolm Fellows. Mr. William Rockefeller, Vice-President. Photo by Evelyn Shafer.

While the number of champions finished each year has risen steadily, the rate of growth, dependent as it is partly on the number of shows and the point scales in the different areas, has perhaps not been quite so spectacular as the growth rate of registrations.

The Westminster Kennel Club Show, first held in 1877, is the two-day show held early in February at New York City. It has become what is surely considered America's most prestigious show.

Twice an Old English Sheepdog has been selected as Best-in-Show at Westminster, and other OES have several other times been close (Group First). It was in 1914 that Ch. Slumber, a bitch owned by Mrs. Tyler Morse's Beaver Brook Kennels, made it to the top of an entry of 1,721 dogs. The judge, Mr. Midgely Marsden, is reported to have said of her that she was the greatest OES of all time, and that he had never seen a dog of any breed that more closely resembled its breed Standard. Ch. Slumber was also a quarter of the Best-in-Show Team at that show.

The only other OES to achieve Best-in-Show at Westminister was Ch. Sir Lancelot of Barvan, bred and owned by Mr. and Mrs. R. Vanword of Newmarket, Ontario, Canada (Tarawoods Beau Billy D x Tarawood's Mistee Weather), who took the top honor in

1975. The judge, Mr. Harry T. Peters, was quoted as calling him "the most magnificent representative of the breed I've ever seen . . . a great mover."

The other OES bitches recorded as Best-of-Breed at Westminster were: Ch. May Morn Weather (1921), Ch. Kinnelon Hallowe'en (1923), Avoca Snowbound (1924), Ch. Donna of Cliffwold (1925), Ch. Lassie of The Farm (1929), and Ch. Mistress Patience of Pastorale (1935).

After its early days in this country, the breed's popularity fell into a decline. In 1926, for example, there were only six OES entered at Westminster. From about 1931 until about 1950, the club was apparently inactive and Specialties were not held for a time. During World War II and up until the 1950s, the breed was kept alive in this country by a few eastern fanciers.

The most rapid rise in popularity of the breed here has occurred in the last ten years. To a certain extent, it may be attributed to the fact that OES were featured in movies and TV, with advertisers picking up the ball from there, so that the public exposure created the demand for puppies. A glance at the AKC registrations statistics reveals the trend and suggests that we may possibly have reached a peak and be leveling off, though at one point the increase was astounding. In 1958 there were only 106 individual registrations of OES, but ten years later the annual individual registrations numbered 2,522. By 1973 the number had increased to 14,751, and in 1974 to 16,050. The rate of increase far exceeded the rate experienced in total purebred dog registrations during the same period. In the past ten years the OES has risen in popularity from about fiftieth place among all breeds to twenty-first place in 1975.

Yet if one dare hazard any conclusion from pictures alone, I think that on the whole, remarkably little change has taken place between the best dogs shown in the earlier years and now, unless perhaps it is that in the United States today the dogs are no longer, as a rule, shown at such advanced ages as they were at the turn of the century. Further, they are presented somewhat differently so far as grooming is concerned. There seems to have been a greater tendency abroad to present the dog naturally as in earlier times (that is, with much less scissor trimming), so that he has more of the shaggy, rugged appearance than we have been accustomed to seeing in the American show rings the past few years.

The following is a summary of milestones in OES history in the United States:

1874—Chicago, June 2, claimed to be the earliest American dog show. (No prizes or awards.) An AKC story (*Gazette*, March, 1974) credits a Chicago show in 1876 as the first under English bench-show rules. Most were informal, irregular affairs at first. No record yet of an OES entry.

1877—First Westminster Show.

1879—First U. S. stud record published (Rowe's *National American Kennel Club Register,* Vol. I)

1883—*American Kennel Register* begins (monthly). It will continue for five volumes.

1884—The American Kennel Club organized (revises By-laws and Rules 1885). The beginning of licensed shows and uniform regulations.

1885—First recorded OES win (Miscellaneous Class), October 6, by "Bob" at Philadelphia. First American-bred litter (Bob x Judith) recorded.

1886—First OES placement (Second) at Westminster (Miscellaneous Class) by "Sir Lucifer." "Bob" registered as No. 3163, first OES in the *American Kennel Register* (January) (not AKC official registration).

1887—The AKC takes over Rowe's Stud Register and continues registrations. In "Bobtailed Sheepdog" Class, Hornellsville, New York, "Sir Lucifer" places First.

1888—(Old English Sheepdog Club founded in England and Standard adopted.)

1889—AKC *Gazette* begins publication (official records only). *Turf, Field, and Farm* publishes an article on the OES by Freeman Lloyd. It was solicited and paid for by Mr. William Wade of Pittsburgh, a wealthy industrialist.

1894—(First OESC Specialty in England.)

1896—First OES kennel prefix registered by Thomas Terry, *Hempstead,* Long Island. Also registered were *Woodlawn Park* by Colonel A. B. Hilton, and *Wellesbourne* by Dr. Henry Jarrett of Chestnut Hill Kennels in Pennsylvania.

1898—AKC registers first OES, a dog, "Gillie," owned by J. Pierpont Morgan's kennel.

1903—H. A. Tilley of Shepton Kennel in England comes to Westminster with entries. First separate classes for OES at Westminster (?). Mr. Tilley stimulates interest in the breed in America.

1904—Mr. Tilley returns to Westminster, a successful exhibitor. He helps to begin organization of an American breed club. First

AKC champions in OES: *Ch. Lady Stumpie* and *Ch. Potsford Bob*.

1905—Old English Sheepdog Club of America recognized by AKC and Standard adopted. There are ten members.

1907—*Dogs* by G. A. Melbourne, an American publication, carries a description of the OES written by J. Freeman Lloyd and illustrated with a picture of Ch. Stylish Boy, among others.

1914—OES is Best-in-Show at Westminster, a bitch, *Ch. Slumber,* owned by Mrs. Tyler Morse. A stud fee of $30.00 for OES "Farmer's Pride" is advertised by Mrs. Thos. W. Larsen of Viking Kennels, Newburgh, New York. (This latter merely an item of passing interest for comparison, for neither the dog nor the owner figures prominently in breed records.)

1921—First OESCA Specialty Show. The OESCA is the first American breed club to hold its Specialty in the classes of a regular all-breed show.

1926—Breed Standard revised to limit maximum height in breed to twenty-six inches.

1930—Sixty-one entries at OESCA Specialty. (By the 1950s, interest has declined so much that for a few years the club does not hold its Specialty.)

1953—OESCA adopts revision of their Breed Standard, approved by AKC, which removes the twenty-six inch maximum limit that had been adopted in 1926.

1970—September 19, first OESCA Independent National Specialty at Anaheim, California, has 165 entries, at that time the largest entry of Old English Sheepdogs in the history of the breed.

1974—Independent Specialty (OESCA) at Buena Park, California, September 21, has 175 dogs with 190 entries.

1975—The OES *Ch. Sir Lancelot of Barvan,* a Canadian dog, takes Best-in-Show at Westminster. The OESCA meeting votes to condemn scissor-sculpturing and other unauthorized show grooming practices and advocates a more natural presentation of the breed in the ring.

Mommy tries to get away from it all.

Deardre's Pashunate Prunella, CDX, owned by Dr. and Mrs. Sheldon Rennert, at about five months.

A Junior Showmanship winner. Ch. Fezziwig Raggety Anne with Junior Margareth Anne Boyer (1968).

Pillars of the Breed

In tracing a pedigree back for a number of generations, one may be astounded to discover that in twelve generations (roughly thirty to forty years) back of any individual Old English Sheepdog (counting the sire and dam as the first generation back), there are 8,190 entries in the list of progenitors. Surely a number of the long-ago great OES would appear back in the line of every living OES today. And so it is that in many cases our American dogs' pedigrees can readily be completed for at least portions of their remote lines back to one or more of the early pillars of the breed.

We do not have much specific information about most of the early ones, even the greatest ones, beyond a very few words written by early fanciers and some barely adequate old pictures of some of them. Of course in each case their direct influence on the present generation is minimal, but they did set the patterns, nevertheless.

It is a far more controversial undertaking to attempt any qualitative report on present-day great dogs, even if one could base it solely on show records (and hence on the opinion of qualified judges). In all fairness, such a statistical basis should be adjusted for many variables such as number of entries, relative quality of the competition, or the records of their progeny.

Some of the pillars of the breed from both the dim past and the present are remarkable for certain of their qualities that were passed along to their numerous progeny, while others are remembered primarily for their own show records; in a few outstanding cases it is for both. Then, too, in looking back at the early dogs, and to some extent even at some of the modern great OES, it is difficult in writing about them to decide whether one should concentrate on the individual dogs themselves, on the breeders who produced a number of them through the years, or on the owners who eventually brought each of them along to success. My method here will be a compromise, or a combination of all three approaches.

Left, Bob-tailed Sheepdog. Ch. Sir Cavendish. Whelped 1887 and prominent among the early English champions, he was referred to in Aubrey Hopwood's book (1905) as "that sterling good dog."

Right, Ch. Watchboy. Breeder, R. Abbott. By Stracathro Bounding Bob ex Nellie II (1890). Grandsire of Ch. Stylish Boy through Young Watch, a three-generation trio that appears among the remote progenitors of a major portion of our breed today.

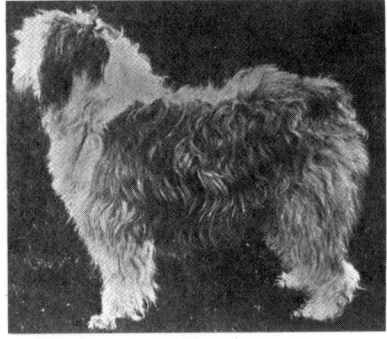

Left, Eng/Amr Ch. Dolly Gray. Whelped 1901 in England and descended through both her sire and dam from Ch. Watchboy, she was the winner in 1903 and 1904 of the Vanderbilt Cup at Westminster. American owner, James A. Garland.

Right, Wall-Eyed Bob. Whelped about 1883 to 1885, his origin is unknown. His wall-eye and correct coat were passed down to successive generations. Owner, Mrs. Fare Fosse, a well-known early days breeder.

When Dr. Edwardes-Ker, Mr. Freeman Lloyd, the Tilley Brothers, and other English breeders began exporting dogs to America, they sent over some which were already eminent among the breed in England; so for a time, at least, we find some of the outstanding early Sheepdogs pre-eminent in both the English and American records of shows and breeding. A considerable number of these dogs and their records are listed in other books on the breed, but among the early ones most often mentioned are the following:

Wall-Eyed Bob. His first owner was J. Thomas, although his origin is unknown. He was sold to Mrs. Fare Fosse, an eminent early breeder in England who bred him to her *Wall-Eyed Flo.* He is credited with transmitting the wall-eye to many later generations of the breed. Probably whelped about 1885, he was a winner at shows until June, 1898, the year of his death. A picture of him bears an original imprint "Bob-tail Sheep dog."

Ch. Fairweather. (Breeder-owner: Mrs. Fosse by Sir James x Birthday, 1898.) A granddaughter of Wall-Eyed Bob through her dam, this bitch had a record of show wins that was unequaled for many years (nineteen Challenge Certificates), and this was a day when there were far fewer shows than there are today. The art of taxidermy preserved her for exhibit at an English museum. Mrs. Fosse, incidentally, was the first woman President of the breed club in England, and hers was the "Weather" kennel strain that did so much to popularize the breed and to leave an imprint of quality in many pedigree lines. It was she who gave us one of the best descriptions of the correct OES coat, something for which her dogs were perhaps best known: "A hard, shaggy coat, not curly or straight (which is worse), but broken in disposition—that is, with just one twist in the hair, as two twists make a curl."

Sir Cavendish. (Breeder: Dr. Edwardes-Ker by Caradoc x Dame Ruth, May, 1887.) A winner 1890-92 inclusive, his picture (a drawing) was used in 1890 to illustrate the breed in Rawdon Lee's book *The Collie or Sheepdog.* The drawing shows the dog in rather short coat and makes him look remarkably like Reinagle's painting published in 1803. He was owned by Dr. Lock (also recorded as Locke). Aubrey Hopwood referred to him in his book as "that sterling good dog."

Ch. Bouncing Lass. (Breeder: E. Y. Butterworth by Young Watch x Peggy Primrose, June 18, 1899.) Mr. H. A. Tilley of Shepton Kennels records that he purchased this bitch from C. W. Macbeth and at the time considered her the best puppy he had ever seen. After numerous wins, including eleven Best-in-Show prizes, he brought her to America in 1903, where she was Best of Opposite Sex, and during the return home she was bred to Ch. Stylish Boy. Later that year he sold her to Mr. Charles Frohman in America on the basis of her picture and his assurance that she could win the Vanderbilt Cup. All but one of her litter returned to the United States with her. After winning the Vanderbilt Cup she was presented to Mr. Reginald Vanderbilt and retired from competition.

Ch. Dolly Gray. (Breeder: Mrs. F. Travis by Stylish Boy x Dolly Daydream, April 26, 1901.) Owned by the Tilleys, she was a champion in both England and America. (Mr. Tilley refers to her as an "International" Champion, but I think we must now interpret that term as then meaning an English/American Championship.) Winner in England of numerous prizes and nine Bests-in-Show in four years, she won the Vanderbilt Cup in America in 1903 and 1904. Mr. Tilley wrote that "her colour, coat, and eyes could not have been more perfect . . . her stance and shortness of back were excellent features." A picture of her suggests that she had a good high rear, too, and a lovely white front and collar, with probably at least one dark ear. She was descended through both her sire and her dam from Ch. Watchboy (also found as Watch Boy). She was sold about 1905 or 1906 to Mr. James A. Garland of New York, whose widow moved his kennels to a farm at Providence, Rhode Island, and briefly continued the successful exhibiting begun by Garland.

This young fancier enjoys the companionship of playful puppies owned by Ken and Meg Crump.

Fezziwig Ceiling Zero and Fezziwig Blackeyed Susan at four and a half weeks, shown in the OESCA trophy for Best of Opposite Sex won by their dam, Ch. Patchwork Gillian of Van R, in 1957.

Ch. Loyalblu Raisin Caine at ten weeks (top), ten months (above), and as a mature "Special" (below), handled by Breeder-Owner Mrs. Linda Jordan.

Brentwood Hero.

Ch. Home Farm Country Lass.

Ch. Stylish Boy.

Frohman and Dillingham's Team of Champions.

Ch. Stylish Boy. (Breeders: Messrs. Potts and Shepherd by Young Watch x Larkfield Watch Lass, September 4, 1898.) He is recorded as owned by F. H. Travis but was brought to America by Mr. Tilley in 1903, returned to England, and was subsequently sold to Charles Frohman and Charles B. Dillingham in America. They are reported to have paid $10,000 for him and three bitches. He was himself one of the early American champions and sire of three others among the first fifteen in this country. When Froham and Dillingham's kennel burned, they gave the dog to Mr. Reginald Vanderbilt. His all-white head was passed down to numerous progeny both in England and America. His sire, Young Watch, and grandsire, Ch. Watchboy, both reportedly had nearly all-white heads. It is said that ninety-eight percent of all Sheepdogs alive today can be traced back to this trio, and Ch. Stylish Boy himself is credited with having more influence on the breed than any other Sheepdog of his era. Mr. Tilley wrote that Mr. Travis, the English owner, was an excellent breeder who stressed "quality, character, and bright skyblue color of coat."

English Ch. Shepton Laddie. (Breeders: Tilley Brothers by Shepton Matchless x Shepton Violet.) Winner of sixteen Challenge Certificates, he was considered by his breeder to be one of the finest specimens he ever bred. His owner, Mrs. Oakman, is said by Mr. Tilley to have refused an offer of one thousand pounds for him (multiply that by five for the dollar equivalent in those days). His measurements, given by Mr. Tilley, were twenty-eight inches at the shoulder and weight of one hundred pounds, which would make him slightly taller than most of our show dogs today. A painting shows him as having an all-white front and collar and nearly all-white head.

Two early top-producing studs owned by Mr. and Mrs. Tyler Morse's Beaver Brook Kennels were *Ch. Shepton Hero* (breeders: Tilley Brothers by Lord Cedric x Avalon Lass, March 24, 1905), who was imported in 1909 and who was Winner's Dog at Westminster in 1910; and his son, *Ch. Brentwood Hero* (x Brentwood Country Girl, April 22, 1908), who was imported by Morse in 1911 and was Winner's Dog at Westminster in 1913, 1915, and 1918 (the last at ten years of age). Ch. Brentwood Hero was the only OES ever to win over the bitch *Ch. Slumber,* his kennel mate.

The Tyler Morse "Beaver Brook" dogs were dominant in the breed at Westminster from 1908 to 1918, winning Best-of-Breed every year except 1911, taking Best-in-Show in 1914, and Reserve Best-in-Show (a designation no longer made) in 1915 and 1916.

All-time Top-Producing OES Sire, winner of fifteen Bests-in-Show, Ch. Fezziwig Ceiling Zero. Breeders-Owners, Hendrik and Serena Van Rensselaer.

Ch. John Marksman, UD(T), first triple-crown OES in obedience, 1946. Owned by the late Fred LaCrosse of Wellesley, Massachusetts, he was outstanding in the breed ring as well. Note the correct wave or "break" in the coat.

Recent American Old English Sheepdogs of Note

It has already been noted that from the 1930s until the 1950s the Old English Sheepdog was temporarily at a low point in popularity in America with fewer than one hundred individual registrations annually, though fortunately a few fanciers in the East were continuing their interest in a quiet way. It was during this period that one of our breed accomplished a remarkable feat in obedience.

Ch. John Marksman. (Breeder-owner: Fred LaCrosse of Wellesley, Massachusetts, by Playboy Clem x Blue Suesanna, November 6, 1940.) A winner in both conformation and obedience, he took Best-in-Show from the American-Bred Class at Bridgewater, Massachusetts, on September 7, 1946. More remarkable, however, is the fact that he was the first OES to complete all three of the obedience degrees, the CD and CDX in 1942, and the UD in 1946. In those days tracking work was a part of the third obedience level, so perhaps he should, by present standards, be listed as a UDT. His photograph shows a very good-looking head and strong body. His coat, with a discernible wave or "break," reminds one of the "Harkaway" and "Weather" coats from other old photos.

Just beginning in 1932 was a new kennel (later to be registered as Fezziwig Kennels) owned by Hendrik and Serena Van Rensselaer, whose dogs would establish and break numerous breed records in the 1960s when Sheepdogs were beginning their rapid rise in popularity. It might fairly be said, I think, that what Shepton dogs were at one time to the British Sheepdogs, Fezziwig dogs have proved to be to American Sheepdogs.

Ch. Fezziwig Ceiling Zero. (Breeders-Owners: the Van Rensselaers, Basking Ridge, New Jersey, by American and Canadian Ch. Farleydene Bartholomew x Ch. Patchwork Gillian of Van R, March 1957.) This is unquestionably the premier dog in the recent-day history of the breed in this country. A whole book could be written about the incredible record of this dog and his numerous equally incredible offspring, for most of the other

Ch. Fezziwig Raggedy Andy, winner of eighteen Bests-in-Show, won the OESCA Challenge Cup six times. Three times placed in Breed, Group, and All-Breed Top Ten (1964-65-66). Breeders-Owners, Hendrik and Serena Van Rensselaer.

Ch. Langley Snowmaiden winning her record-breaking nineteenth Best-in-Show under Judge Winifred Heckman at Fort Myers, November 17, 1973. Trophy presented by Club President Josie A. Mitchell. Handled by Don Bradley for Owners Kathy and Ben Bedford, Jr.

American-bred record-making Sheepdogs of recent years are his descendants or are descended from one or both of his parents.

Winner of fifteen Bests-in-Show, at the end of 1974 he still headed the list of sires of champions with an astounding sixty-three champion get which carry as many as thirty kennel prefixes in their names. One of his sons, Ch. Rivermist Dan Patch, exceeded his father's show record with seventeen Bests-in-Show. Ceilie is remembered, as well, for being the sire of the record nine-champion litter (see below), several of whom were Westminster, Specialty, and Best-in-Show winners like their sire and dam. Ceilie was four times Best-of-Breed at Westminster and three times Best-of-Breed at OESCA Specialties. He and several of his sons (including Dan Patch) were leading sires in this country at the time of the recent spectacular rise in breed registrations. He died in 1969.

Ch. Fezziwig Raggedy Andy. (Breeders-owners: the Van Rensselaers by American and Canadian Ch. Farleydene Bartholomew x Ch. Fezziwig Blackeyed Susan.) This dog was a kennel mate of Ceilie's and closely related to him, his sire being the same and his dam being a litter sister of Ceilie's. Until 1973, Raggedy Andy held the record for Bests-in-Show by an OES (eighteen), including such prestigious shows as Detroit, Baltimore, Chicago International, and Greenwich. In three years he was three times each Best-of-Breed at Westminster (twice going on to Group First) and at OESCA Specialties, winning the OESCA Challenge Cup six times.

Ch. Langley Snowmaiden. (Ch. Fezziwig Vice Versa x Fezziwig Bonnie Blue Belle.) (Owners: Kathy and Ben Bedford, Jr., of Chattanooga, Tennessee.) One of Ceilie's descendants (a great-granddaughter), this bitch is the all-time Best-in-Show OES and on her sire's side is a fourth generation Best-in-Show winner. She is descended back of her dam from Ceilie through Ch. Fezziwig Fringe Benefits, and back of her sire, from Ceilie's sire through Ch. Fezziwig Raggedy Andy. "Dolly" was campaigned extensively for only eighteen months, and in 1973 she became the first OES bitch ever to place in all three categories of the top ten (All-Breed Eighth, Working Group Fifth, and Breed First). Her Best-in-Show record was nineteen.

Another Ceilie descendant of note is *Ch. Prince Andrew of Sherline* (breeder: Mrs. D. C. Swanson by Ch. Shagbourne's Messenger x Shepton Mistress Mary), owned by Mr. Howard Sherline and his wife, the late Mrs. Rita Sherline. A grandson of Ceilie through his sire, he was Best-of-Breed at two Eastern Club Specialties (1968

Ch. Tempest of Dalcroy, Tamara Kennels' Register of Merit Sire, produced twenty-one champions. Owners, Mr. and Mrs. Marvin Smith.

Ch. Chatsworth Mister Higgins, Top OES Male, 1972, shown taking Working Group First, handled by Ray McNulty for Owners Dr. Wilks O. Hiatt, Jr., and Natalie Hiatt.

and 1969) and twice at Westminster (1969 and 1970), as well as being the top-ranked OES for three years (1968-1970).

To go into any detail in describing any of these dogs is merely to describe the Standard. It is difficult to recall many top-winning OES in the past ten years in this country that have even approached these records that are not either related to these dogs in some degree or imported. One should not, however, overlook a number of other excellent dogs by emphasizing with superlatives the records of a few top winners that may have been campaigned most extensively. It may not be fair, either, to compare the winning records of any two or more dogs without taking into account as well any number of such contributing factors as their number of entries, the particular places where they won, the relative quality of their competition, and the number of different judges who saw them.

An imported dog that has figured prominently both in winning and in producing winners in recent years is *English and American Ch. Prospect Blue Rodger,* owned by Mrs. Mona Berkowitz of Thousand Oaks, California. Ranked Number Two OES in 1969 and 1970, he was twice an OESCA Specialty winner, and his son, *Ch. Dustmop's St. Nicholas* (x Ch. Rivermist March Flower) owned by Terry and Kathy Crow of Vermillion, South Dakota, was Number Three OES in 1972 and 1973. "Nicky" was the breed winner at Westminster in 1973 and 1974, as well as a Best-in-Show winner. Through his dam, he was also descended from Ceilie.

Outstanding among others recently is *Ch. Chatsworth Mister Higgins* (Ch. Tempest of Dalcroy x Ch. Lady Chatterly of Wragby, August 27, 1968, breeders-owners: Dr. and Mrs. Wilks O. Hiatt, Jr., Raleigh, North Carolina). His sire, one of Tamara Kennel's imports, better known as "Harvey," was one of the all-time top-producing sires in this country. Though not extensively campaigned, Higgins was the top male among Sheepdogs (Number Two among OES, Phillips System) in 1972. Shown twenty-eight times that year, he was twice Best-in-Show and seventeen times Best-of-Breed (followed fourteen times by Group wins or placements). He has been praised especially for his excellent movement, but is difficult to fault in any significant respect, and several of his puppies are showing considerable promise in the ring.

Two early world breeding records for the number of champions from one litter were held by OES. In Sheepdogs, at least, they were surpassed in America by Barry Goodman's litter (Ch. Fezziwig Ceiling Zero x Ch. Baroness of Duroya), whelped May 5,

Ch. Loyalblu Hendihap Templeton with Breeder Linda Jordan handling under Judge Deedy Abrams at Louisiana Kennel Club (entry ninety-three) going Best of Winners.

1964, at his Rivermist Kennels at Bethesda, Maryland, which produced nine champions. The sire and dam had been Best of Breed and Best of Opposite Sex at Westminster and at OESCA Specialties, wins that were repeated among them by two dogs and three bitches from the litter. A tenth litter mate, Rivermist Heather, came close to attaining a championship as well. Several of the champions from the litter also themselves produced numerous top-winning progeny. The record-making champions from the litter were: Ch. Rivermist Dan Patch, Ch. Rivermist Marco Polo, Ch. Rivermist Galahad, Ch. Rivermist Gulliver, Ch. Rivermist Gentian (bitch), Ch. Rivermist Nosegay (bitch), Ch. Rivermist Hollyhock (bitch), Ch. Rivermist Bellflower (bitch), and American and Canadian Ch. Rivermist Indigo, CD (bitch). Dan Patch, Marco Polo, Galahad, Gentian, Hollyhock, and Indigo were top winners at shows.

Top-winning Old English Sheepdogs in the United States (1963-1973) who ranked (Phillips System) in both Working Group and All-Breed lists of the top ten were:

   1963—Ch. Fezziwig Ceiling Zero (the Van Rensselaers)
   1964—Amr/Can Ch. Tarawood's Blue Baron (Estate of Adelene Isakson)
   1964—Ch. Fezziwig Raggedy Andy (the Van Rensselaers)
   1965—Ch. Fezziwig Raggedy Andy
   1966—Ch. Fezziwig Raggedy Andy
   1967—Ch. Rivermist Dan Patch (Mr. and Mrs. Howard Payne)
   1968—Ch. Prince Andrew of Sherline (Mr. and Mrs. Howard Sherline)
   1969—Ch. Prince Andrew of Sherline
   1973—Ch. Langley Snowmaiden (B) (Mr. and Mrs. Ben Bedford, Jr.)

Among the OES with all-breed Best-in-Show wins (other than those mentioned previously in this chapter) during the period 1963-1975 are:

Ch. Bahlamb's Brazen Bandit (J. Wexler and Caj Haakansson)
Ch. Baroness of Duroya (B) (Mr. and Mrs. Barry Goodman)
Bramshed's Lady Guinevere (Dr. P. C. Feinberg)
Ch. Brooks Blue Boy (Miss Florence Pangborn)
Ch. Driftwood's Oliver Twist, CD (J. and R. Murphy)
Amr/Can Ch. Droverdale Image of Polo (Mrs. Sandi Baker)
Ch. Fezziwig Artful Dodger (Hendrik and Serena Van Rensselaer)
Ch. Fezziwig Bartholomew (Dr. and Mrs. Oren Bush)
Ch. Fezziwig Fringe Benefits (Hendrik and Serena Van Rensselaer)
Ch. Fezziwig Vice Versa (Hendrik and Serena Van Rensselaer)
Ch. Happy Hay Crumpet (B) (J. A. and S. M. Manning and W. K. Perry)
Ch. Leach's Puff 'N Stuff (J. S. Sturgill)
Ch. Loyalblu Hendihap (Dr. and Mrs. Hugh Jordan)
Ch. Mitepa's Burhead Kid (Dr. and Mrs. Oren Bush)
Ch. Momarv's Bruno Boy Hayseed (Mrs. Mona Berkowitz)
Ch. Morrow's Christopher Beowulf (Miss K. Raffery)
Ch. Morrow's Duke of Fuzzbuzz (I. and R. Forbes)
Eng/Amr Ch. Prospect Blue Rodger (Mrs. Mona Berkowitz)
Ch. Rivermist Galahad (H. H. Hecht, Jr.)
Ch. Shaggybar Bottomsup (Stan Goldberg)
Ch. Shaggiluv Checkmate (A. S. and D. Karson)
Ch. Silvershag Snowblaze (Dr. C. A. Waterbury)
Amr/Can Ch. Sir Lancelot of Barvan (Mr. and Mrs. Ronald Vanword)

Ch. Fezziwig Vice Versa, top winner at the OESCA Specialty, October, 1973, was an outstanding OES and the sire of Ch. Langley Snowmaiden, who holds the OES record for Bests-In-Show. Breeders-Owners, Hendrik and Serena Van Rensselaer.

"Bumble," bred and owned by the Author.

Deardre's Once In A Blue Moon, CD, at seven months. Owners, Dr. and Mrs. Sheldon Rennert.

Ch. Shaggywonder Prince Charming ("Boomer"), Tamara Kennels' sire of twelve champions.

Ch. Fezziwig Bartholomew, First in Group, Heart of America Kennel Club, 1966, where he went on to Best in Show. Owners, Dr. and Mrs. Oren D. Bush. Judge, Mr. Plaga. Handler, Philip Hofeld. Trophy presenter, Mrs. Leonard Rubenitz. Note long, untrimmed coat in 1966.

The following are other Sheepdogs not already mentioned but nevertheless among those on the lists of noteworthy breed winners and (some of them) producers of several champions. (Author's note: To omit any OES from this list is to slight the favorite of many individuals, and may I be forgiven for doing so in each such case.)

Ch. B & H's Holiday Showcase (H. Schmid and R. Beckert)
*Ch. Barrelroll Blues in the Night (W. B. Garvey and Sherman Katz)
*Ch. Bobtail Acres Rough 'N Ready (M. L. and R. K. Short)
*Ch. Double JJ's Uncle Sam (Peter J. Entringer)
Ch. Downeylane Donnybrook, CD (Mrs. Robert Abrams, Jr.)
Ch. Duke Karl of Brunswick (C. Geiger)
Amr/Can Ch. Echo Valley Tidleywink (Dr. and Mrs. Oren Bush)
*Ch. Fezziwig Hidden Assets (Anna Jacobson and Serena Van Rensselaer)
*Ch. Knightcap's Moody Blue (Joseph and Douglas Caroli)
Ch. Momarv's Snooper Sleuth (Mrs. Mona Berkowitz)
Ch. Nestledowns Mr. Tough Guy (Don Reid)
Ch. Professor of Greyfriar (Dr. and Mrs. Oren Bush)
*Amr/Can Ch. Rivermist Dan Tatters (Bob and Sheila Ziccardi and Jim McTernan)
*Amr/Can Ch. Rivermist Feather Merchent, CD (Dr. and Mrs. Gary Carter)
*Ch. Rivermist Hornblower (Dr. and Mrs. W. R. Snider)
Ch. Shaggy Wonder Prince Charming (Mrs. Marvin Smith)
*Ch. Shandy Kip London (C. G. and J. E. Marshall)
Ch. Shayloran's Billy Hayseed (Mrs. Mona Berkowitz)
*Amr/Can Ch. Squarecote Fogbound (Mr. and Mrs. David Lee)
*Ch. Sugar Creek Serjeant Buzfuz (M. J. Amweg)
*Ch. Sunnybrae Jack Frost (Major and Mrs. Robert F. Lopina)
Ch. Tamara's Shaggy Shoes MacDuff (D. and J. McColl)
*Ch. Tamara's Smokey of Bishop (Mrs. Marvin Smith)
Ch. Tempest of Dalcroy (Mrs. Marvin Smith)
(*) Descendants of "Ceilie"

Ch. Prospectblue Samuel, Loyalblu Kennels' import, going Winners Dog for five point major at Golden Gate Kennel Club Show.

Ch. Tamara's Patches of Perse, dam of nine champions, at home in Brighton, Michigan. Note the untrimmed, "natural" look of past years. This picture shows the natural wave or "break" of the proper coat (not curly).

Amr/Can Ch. Silvermist Peek-a-Boo finishing in Canada under Judge Pat Randall, owner-handled by Anne Weisse. The twenty-month-old bitch is beginning to show some adult coat.

Top-winning bitches Ch. Langley Snowmaiden (Kathy and Ben Bedford, Jr.), Ch. Rivermist Hollyhock (Barry Goodman), Ch. Rivermist Indigo, CD (B. W. and J. M. Kohler), and Ch. Baroness of Duroya (Barry Goodman) have already been mentioned. However, since few bitches achieve top-winning records (partly because they are retired early to concentrate on motherhood and also because they normally cannot win over a good dog), we must more often recognize their contribution to breed records through tabulating the number of champions they have produced. High in the ranks in this category in recent years are:

Miss Muffett of Tatters (Gail Janoff)
Ch. Patchwork Gillian of Van R (Hendrik and Serena Van Rensselaer)
Ch. Rivermist Nosegay (Barry Goodman and Nancy Miller)
Ch. Rivermist Gentian (F. E. and E. H. Rich)
Ch. Tamara's Patches of Perse (Mrs. Marvin Smith)
Ch. Silvershag Ruffles (Dr. Louise Forest)
Ch. Beckington Aristocrat (Mrs. Lillian Lovejoy)
Ch. Silvershag Donnemerry (Sandi Baker and Mr. and Mrs. Stebbins)
Ch. Silvershag Frolic (Dr. Louise Forest)
Ch. Silvershag Sweet Sue (Hendrik and Serena Van Rensselaer)
Ch. Jendower's Queen Victoria (Gail H. Fletcher)
Rivermist Heather (Mrs. J. Hammerel and Mrs. J. Anderson)
Gloria's Own Callistopee (Harriet Poreda)

Shelly Smith receiving the annual OESCA Junior Handler Trophy from Mrs. Mona Berkowitz for 1973. Mrs. Robert Abrams, Jr., OESCA Junior Showmanship Chairman, looks on. Shelly qualified for the Junior Finals at West-minster and competed there in 1974. Mrs. Berkowitz won the Junior Finals at Westminster in 1939 showing an OES.

Ch. Mitepa's Burhead Kid taking Group First at Tulsa, Oklahoma (1973). Owned and handled by Dr. Oren Bush. Note the sculptured appearance scissored in 1973. One of America's Top Ten OES in 1974.

In her 1961 breed handbook, Mrs. Jill Keeling listed forty-three British kennel name prefixes together with the owners' names. In 1973, the *Bobtail Directory,* published in Wales by David Miller and John Winter, listed one hundred current British "prefix holders" with names and addresses, and only ten of them had previously appeared also in Mrs. Keeling's list. Allowing for the probability of a few accidental oversights, this still represents a remarkable increase in a twelve-year period, as well as the apparent retirement of a number of the early well-known kennel names, assuming they had ever been registered with the Kennel Club as "prefix holders."

Among the best-known British kennel names found in the backgrounds of many of our present American dogs and among recent American imports are: Beckington, Bewkes, Boldwood, Dalcroy, Danum, Duroya, Fairacres, Farleydene, Fernville, Greystoke, Loakes Park, Marlay, Pastelblue, Pendlefold, Prospectblue, Reculver, Rollingsea, Shepton, Somerstreet, Squarefour, Tansley, Twotrees, Watchers, Weather, and Weirwood.

Loyalblu Kennels' Ch. Seekapetra Seamist. This English-bred dog won breeds from the classes and as a "Special."

Ch. Fezziwig Raggedy Andy at home in Basking Ridge, New Jersey, checks for more "fan mail."

Ch. Fezziwig Ceiling Zero and Ch. Fezziwig Blackeyed Susan dressed for show.

Among American kennels producing the greater number of champions and/or breed high-score (Phillips System) dogs in recent years are:

Ambelon, Anne M. Raker, Lincoln, Massachusetts
Bahlamb, Mr. Caj Haakasson, Wheaton, Maryland
Barnstorm, Joe McAskill, Long Grove, Illinois
Bear Creek, Mr. and Mrs. James Mattern, East Lansing, Michigan
Bobtail Acres, Mr. and Mrs. John Herlihy, El Cajon, California
Chatsworth, Dr. and Mrs. Wilks O. Hiatt, Jr., Raleigh, North Carolina
Dogpatch, Mr. and Mrs. W. C. Mowell, Knoxville, Tennessee
Double JJ, Joyce M. Anderson, Bigelow, Minnesota
Downeylane, Mrs. Robert Abrams, Jr., Kansas City, Missouri
Droverdale, Mr. and Mrs. Pat Baker, San Francisco, California
Echo Valley, Mrs. Norma J. Rockwell, Oxford, Michigan
Fezziwig, Mr. and Mrs. Hendrik Van Rensselaer, Basking Ridge, New Jersey
Fogbound, Mr. and Mrs. Charles Geiger, West Chicago, Illinois
Greyfriar, Mrs. Harriet Poreda, Lakewood, Colorado
Ivyridge, Mr. and Mrs. Louis Loeb, Helena, Montana
Jendower, Captain and Mrs. F. E. Rich, Herndon, Virginia
Knightcap, Mrs. Joan Demko, Huntington, New York
Knottingham, Mr. and Mrs. Earl Jacobson, Peoria, Illinois
Lillibrad, Mrs. Lillian Lovejoy, Denver, Colorado
Limey Lane, Susan Davis, Ellicott City, Maryland
Loyalblu, Dr. and Mrs. Hugh Jordan, Whittier, California
Mitepa, Dr. and Mrs. Oren Bush, Oklahoma City, Oklahoma
Momarv, Mrs. Mona Berkowitz, Thousand Oaks, California
Moptop, L. A. Nelson, Merrifield, Virginia
Morrow, Mrs. Mae Marie Morrow, Saint Clair Shores, Michigan
Ragbear, Mrs. Gail H. Fletcher, Phoenix, Arizona
Rivermist, Mr. and Mrs. Barry Goodman, Bethesda, Maryland
Rolling Gait, Mr. and Mrs. Clifford Gheen, Peekskill, New York
Shaggiluv, Mr. and Mrs. Terrance Crow, Vermillion, South Dakota
Silvershag, Dr. Louise Forest, New Hartford, Iowa
Sugar Creek, Mrs. John Albert, Jr., Lima, Ohio
Squarecote, Mr. and Mrs. David Lee, Kent, Washington
Sunnybrae, Ann W. Penn, Hawthorne, Nevada
Tamara, Mrs. Marvin Smith, Brighton, Michigan

(Note: Not all of the kennels listed above are AKC-registered prefixes, nor are all of them still actively breeding at this time.)

The Canadian OES kennels that are probably among the best known in the United States are:

Shayloran, Mr. and Mrs. Harold F. Richards
Some Buddy's, Dr. and Mrs. Gary Carter, Okotoks, Alberta
Tarawood, Mrs. Diane Buckland

Ch. Two Trees Black Eyed Susan (Eng/Amr Ch. Prospect Blue Rodger x Rollingsea Sunbeam) owned by Loyalblu Kennels.

Ch. Tamara's Patches of Perse and Ch. Tempest of Dalcroy, Register of Merit Sire and Dam, by the lake at Tamara Kennels. Both are listed among the All-Time Champion Producing OES, having produced nine and twenty-one champions respectively.

Puppies owned by Betty E. Bradley, Dallas, Texas.

The all-time top champion-producing sires and dams and the total number of champions each has sired are:

Sires	Total Champions (As of 1975)
*Ch. Fezziwig Ceiling Zero	63
*Ch. Unnesta Pim	46
*Ch. Rivermist Dan Tatters	36
*Ch. Fezziwig Vice Versa	29
Ch. Rivermist Danpatch	23
*Ch. Tempest of Dalcroy	21
Ch. Silvershag Snowbright	16
*Ch. Farleydene Bartholomew	15
*Ch. Sandy Kip London	15
*Ch. Prospect Shaggy Boy	14

*—Deceased

Dams	Total Champions (As of 1974)
*Ch. Rivermist Gentian	14
Ch. Rivermist Nosegay	12
Miss Muffit of Tatters	11
*Ch. Patchwork Gillian of Van R	11
*Ch. Baroness of Duroya	9 (one litter)
*Ch. Silvershag Donnemerry	9
*Ch. Silvershag Ruffles	9
*Ch. Tamara's Patches of Perse	9
*Ch. Beckington Aristocrat	8
*Ch. Ragbear Bobmar's Hillary Mist	8

*—Deceased

A clipped Sheepdog and puppies.

Puppy owned by Ken and Meg Crump, with "pal."

Anne Weisse's trio wait off stage for their entrance. "Junior," "Susie," and "Smudge" at Fort Wayne, Detroit, Michigan, 1963.

The Old English Sheepdog breed winners at Westminster Kennel Club Shows since 1965 are:

Year		Winners	Owners
1965	BB:	Ch. Fezziwig Raggedy Andy	Van Rensselaer
	BOS:	Ch. Baroness of Duroya	Goodman
1966	BB:	Ch. Fezziwig Raggedy Andy	Van Rensselaer
	BOS:	*Ch. Rivermist Hollyhock	Goodman
1967	BB:	Ch. Fezziwig Raggedy Andy	Van Rensselaer
	BOS:	*Ch. Rivermist Hollyhock	Goodman
1968	BB:	*Ch. Rivermist Dan Patch	Payne
	BOS:	*Ch. Rivermist Hollyhock	Goodman
1969	BB:	*Ch. Prince Andrew of Sherline	Sherline
	BOS:	*Ch. Knightcap's Fabulous Fanny	Jacobson
1970	BB:	*Ch. Prince Andrew of Sherline	Sherline
	BOS:	Ch. Silvershag Carnival Cut Up	Woehlbing
1971	BB:	*Ch. Brooks Blue Boy	Pangborn
	BOS:	*Ch. Lady Bufferton of Latham	Lutomski
1972	BB:	Ch. Fezziwig Vice Versa	Van Rensselaer
	BOS:	*Ch. Kotton Kandy's Misty Muffet	Kamens
1973	BB:	*Ch. Dustmop's St. Nicholas	Crow
	BOS:	*Ch. Langley Snowmaiden	Bedford
1974	BB:	*Ch. Dustmop's St. Nicholas	Crow
	BOS:	Ch. Silvershag Snowlady Rosalyn	Moulton
1975	BB:	Ch. Sir Lancelot of Barvan (also BIS)	Vanword
	BOS:	*Ch. Hapenny Amazing Grace	Schneider
1976	BB:	*Ch. Raytom's Toby Chuzzlewit	Murray
	BOS:	*Ch. Knottingham's Royal Juliana	Decker
1977	BB:	Ch. Loyalblue Hendihap	Loyalblue Knls. & Boerner
	BOS:	Ch. Tighe's Sheeba of Misty Isles	Gretten

*—Descendant of Ch. Fezziwig Ceiling Zero (the Van Rensselaer dogs Ch. Fezziwig Raggedy Andy and Ch. Fezziwig Vice Versa go back to the sire and dam of "Ceilie")

The Author's Greyfriar Silver Sixpence at eight and a half years in full shaggy array untouched by scissors.

Ch. Prospectblue Elizabeth, Best of Opposite Sex at first Independent Specialty of OESCA, shown here going Best of Breed under English Breeder-Judge Jean Gould. Loyalblu Kennels.

The Old English Sheepdog Club of America Specialty Show winners since 1965 are:

Year and Place	Winners		Owners
1965 Detroit, Mich.	BB: BOS:	Ch. Fezziwig Raggedy Andy Ch. Bonnie Blue of Saltbox	Van Rensselaer Baer
1965 Westbury, Conn.	BB: BOS:	Ch. Fezziwig Raggedy Andy *Ch. Rivermist Gentian	Van Rensselaer Rich
1966 Trenton, N.J.	BB: BOS:	Ch. Fezziwig Raggedy Andy *Ch. Rivermist Indigo, CD	Van Rensselaer Kohler
1966 Kansas City, Mo.	BB: BOS:	Ch. Fezziwig Bartholomew *Ch. Rivermist Hollyhock	Bush Goodman
1967 Westchester, N.Y.	BB: BOS:	*Ch. Rivermist Galahad *Ch. Rivermist Hollyhock	Hecht Goodman
1967 Santa Barbara, Calif.	BB: BOS:	Ch. Shayloran's Billy Hayseed (Imp.) Ch. Nobility Shaggibar Lotablu	Berkowitz Goldberg & Rudholm
1968 Greenwich, Conn.	BB: BOS:	*Ch. Prince Andrew of Sherline *Ch. Rivermist Hollyhock	Sherline Goodman
1969 Chagrin Falls, Ohio	BB: BOS:	*Ch. Knightcap's Moody Blue (D) *Ch. Knightcap's Gimlet (B)	Caroli Demko
1969 Kansas City, Mo.	BB: BOS:	Ch. Prospect Blue Rodger (Imp.) *Ch. Rivermist Sweetbriar	Berkowitz Horton
1969 Atlantic City, N.J.	BB: BOS:	*Ch. Prince Andrew of Sherline *Ch. Fezziwig Daisy Mae	Sherline McCabe
1970 Anaheim, Calif. (Independent)	BB: BOS:	Ch. Prospect Blue Rodger (Imp.) Ch. Prospectblue Elizabeth (Imp.)	Berkowitz Jordan
1970 Grayslake, Ill.	BB: BOS:	*Ch. Droverdale Image of Polo Ch. Silvershag Carnival Cut Up	Baker Woehlbing
1971 Dallas, Tex.	BB: BOS:	*Ch. Droverdale Image of Polo *Ch. Fezziwig Melissa	Baker Keck

Amr/Can Ch. Rivermist Feather Merchent, Can CD, going Best of Breed in California under Judge David Parker at two years. Owned by Dr. and Mrs. Gary Carter of Canada, co-owned by James McTernan. "Friendly" was Top OES in Canada in 1970 and 1971 and Number Four OES in the United States in 1971. At the OESCA Specialty in 1974 he was BOS.

Ch. Fezziwig Ceilie's Blue Print, the last son of Ch. Fezziwig Ceiling Zero at the Van Rensselaers' Fezziwig Kennels.

1971 Greenwich, Conn.	BB: BOS:	Amr/Can Ch. Gwehelog Blue Valley Boy (Imp.) Ch. Tamara's Carole's Folly	Rockwell Phillips
1971 Wellesley, Mass	BB: BOS:	*Amr/Can Ch. Rivermist Feather Merchant, Can CD *Ch. Fezziwig Andorra	Carter Lamb
1972 Wellesley, Mass.	BB: BOS:	Ch. Twotrees Chrysanthemum (B) (Imp.) Ch. Fezziwig Vice Versa (D)	Schneider Van Rensselaer
1972 Ravenna, Ohio (Independent)	BB: BOS:	Ch. Stonebarrow's Friar Tuck *Ch. Kotton Kandy's Misty Muffet	Jones Kamens
1973 New Orleans, La. (Independent)	BB: BOS:	Ch. Fezziwig Vice Versa *Ch. Langley Snowmaiden	Van Rensselaer Bedford
1974 Buena Park, Calif. (Independent)	BB: BOS:	*Amr/Can Ch. Cheerio Ragged Pacesetter (B) * Amr/Can Ch. Rivermist Feather Merchant, Can CD	Samuelson Carter
1975 New Canaan, Conn. (Independent)	BB: BOS:	Ch. Vidmar's Visibility Zero (D) *Ch. Jendower's Cloud Nine (B)	Arble, Moulton & Shepard Rich
1976 Ravenna, Ohio (Independent)	BB: BOS:	Ch. Cheerio Heavy Number *Ch. Deardre's Roxy Music	Leach Arble

*—Descendants of Ch. Fezziwig Ceiling Zero

Christopher Bush will probably learn to walk by holding on to the long coat on Grandpa Oren Bush's Ch. Mitepa's Burhead Kid

Sheepdog puppy meets a lamb.

Brek-Haven Henry of Greyfriar, CDX, in action. He was second highest-scoring OES in Open obedience, 1973. Owners, Ken and Meg Crump.

Deirdre's Heavenly Baby, CD, undergoing training for Open obedience with her handler, Deirdre Rennert. Deirdre was the winner of the first Junior Handler Trophy awarded by the OESCA in 1969 for Junior Showmanship. She now concentrates on obedience work.

The Old English Sheepdog as a Working Dog

While the Bobtail is called a sheepdog, and has surely been employed in instances as a sheepherding dog, he is known primarily as a drover's dog. I find no record that he has customarily been seen competing at any sheepdog trials, though he may have been, on occasions at least. Few of us ever have an opportunity to see an Old English Sheepdog actually at work these days, except possibly in Walt Disney movies, so we must be content with reading about the ones who may still be fulfilling the purpose of the breed.

The late Harold Pike of the Isle of Wight wrote for the *OESCA Bulletin* early in 1973 about the "Smithfield Dogs," explaining that in southern England before the days of paved roads and railway transportation, our Bobtails took sheep and cattle to market on the hoof, often traveling a hundred miles or more on dusty roads where their bear-like ambling gait conserved energy remarkably well. He notes that an old volume on dogs delightfully described the dog's movement as "lollaping along."

The drovers' journey ended at the Smithfield Market at London, stops being made on long trips at inns along the way. As many as twenty to thirty Bobtails were part of the market scene, so they were known in the city as "Smithfield dogs." (It should be noted here that some writers insist that this was not the true purebred Old English Sheepdog but rather a crossbred Beardie.)

At any rate, Mr. Pike records, "During its heyday, the Bobtail had an Inn named after him and this was on a corner near to Smithfield Market. It was called simply 'The Bobtail' . . . Although I once had an old print showing the Inn sign, no trace can be found of the site. The picture on the sign showed a Bobtail alright, although the picture was of an unkempt dog and, quite obviously, it was painted from a real-life drovers dog."

The instinct for herding (or driving) is readily discernible when you see a dam rounding up her puppies in the field or steering them away from dangerous areas. It is also seen among several dogs.

when they want to keep all your attention for themselves and away from one of their number.

While Old English Sheepdogs no longer make the long drives to market these days, many may still be seen on farms in both Britain and America, and often working alone, driving cows between field and barn and back. Mr. H. A. Tilley wrote of several such dogs back in 1933. Of one, he wrote.

"Ben", in charge of a herd or flock, was without fear and had a heart of steel. I have once seen him kicked over by a horse and many times by cows, but beyond a momentary expression of pain and limping for a mile or two, he performed his tasks as if nothing had happened, and with a degree of sagacity which was little short of human . . . Memories of him were long kept green . . . When other dogs were bungling their work, . . . one heard the shepherd or drover remark: "Wants old 'Ben' back again to show 'em 'ow!"

How devoted the farm family was to its Bobtail is exemplified by another of Mr. Tilley's stories. He was offering to buy a likely bitch from a farmer. The farmer called to his wife, "Missus, Mr. Tilley do want to buy our 'Lass'." The instant reply from the house was, "Then you'd better sell I with her."

Mollie Pike reported in the *OESCA Bulletin* on the Bobtail as a guard dog, especially for watching home and children, as follows: "It seems that this great inborn desire to protect has always been present, no matter what strain a Bobtail comes from. It dates back to the days of the early Old English when on many small farms in England, the wife of the farmer would help in the fields alongside her husband. If they had a family, and most of them had large families, the Bobtail would be sent inside to guard the children. And woe to the person who attempted to take advantage of the absence of the parents. They guard children ferociously, and to stop a man entering a house, I have seen a Bobtail stand up on his hind legs and fight a six-foot man, striking out with his front legs like a boxer."

An even more remarkable incident was recounted to me by Mrs. Jocelyn Fedak of Phoenix, Arizona, as follows: "I watched with concern but with curiosity the attempts of our 1½-year-old son, Chio, to progress toward the swimming pool in our yard. Instinctively, it seemed, our OES female was just as determined that he not reach the pool, and she herded him away. After much useless persuasion, 'Aunt Maggie' finally wrapped both her paws round him and ever so gently laid him on the patio, not even so much as bumping his head. Not so keen on this, Chio screamed, kicked, poked, and scratched trying to get up; meanwhile, Maggie patiently held her one paw in the middle of his stomach. When he finally found out that Maggie was the winner, his struggles subsided and she gently let him get up. She then proceeded to herd him back through the sliding glass door into the house and promptly placed herself in the doorway and would not let him out again.''

I do not know what mine would do if they were faced with the necessity of a real defense of any of our family or property, for their size alone has always posed threat enough to assure protection. However, I can testify that the sound of their hysterical barking did quickly frighten off two strange men who were trying to break into our house through the garage one day—and at about the same hour a neighbor's house *was* burglarized!

In obedience competition we can see the modern facsimile of the Bobtail at ''work.'' Recalling my own family's brief flirtation with obedience entries, and observing others in the ring and listening to the stories of the experiences of some of their owners, I would have said that our breed has too much of the puckish, fun-loving Court Jester in it to achieve any notable success in the obedience ring. In some cases, I'm sure this may be true; but my examination of the records while seeking material for this chapter has proved quite the opposite to be the fact.

In the last few years the increase in the number of OES obedience degrees has reflected the increasing growth rate in the breed's

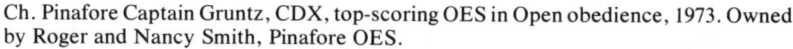

Ch. Pinafore Captain Gruntz, CDX, top-scoring OES in Open obedience, 1973. Owned by Roger and Nancy Smith, Pinafore OES.

Ch. Pinafore Captain Gruntz, CDX, on the way to a First in Open "A" (195) and his second "leg" at Tucson, Arizona, March 4, 1973. Owners, Roger and Nancy Smith, Pinafore OES.

popularity. In 1964, when the individual OES registrations (AKC) were 473, there were only four Old English Sheepdogs who earned a CD, and there were no other OES obedience degrees that year. But the picture steadily improved after that until, in 1975 when there were 15,623 OES registered during the year, there were seventy-eight CD's, ten CDX's, and three UD's finished.

When one realizes that only in the more populous areas, for the most part, does one find available an adequate opportunity to learn to train the dogs for the more advanced degrees, and further, that in advanced obedience work the OES is working at some disadvantage with hair in his eyes, then I think the record of the Bobtail in obedience is quite a creditable one.

In several instances, the scores earned by Old English Sheepdogs on the way to their degrees are good ones, too, and each year they are getting better. Take, for example, the record of the top-scoring OES in Open "A" for the year 1973. Ch. Pinafore Captain Gruntz, CDX, bred and owned by Roger and Nancy Smith of Phoenix, Arizona, was in the ribbons on each of his three CDX qualifying legs:

Sahuaro State K. C.	3/3/73 197½	Tied for First Place
Tucson K. C.	3/4/73 195	First Place
Phoenix Field & Obedience	4/7/73 193½	Second Place

Obedience Open "A" winners at Tucson Kennel Club, March 4, 1973. First place went to Ch. Pinafore Captain Gruntz (then CD) for his second "leg." Owners, Roger and Nancy Smith, Pinafore OES.

He had finished his CD at nine and a half months with scores of 189-190½-192. His kennel mate, Droverdale Pinafore's Winke, earned her CD degree with three consecutive scores of 196½-190-194½. Gruntz' sister, Ch. Pinafore Loverly Penelope, CD, owned by Mr. and Mrs. Dean Cotanche of Tucson, Arizona, was trained and handled to her first obedience degree by a junior handler, Cheryl Cotanche.

Among the High Score Trophy winners at trials in 1975 were: Mother Nature of Beau Cheval, CD (John and Lois Landis), High in Trial (197) from Novice "A" at the Pocono Mountain Kennel Club over twenty-seven dogs; Queen Victoria IV, CD (Annette Heiner), High in Trial (198½) from Novice "A" at the Intermountain Kennel Club over sixty-one dogs; Blueacre Picadilly Pixie, CDX (Yvette Neary), High in Trial (186) from Open "A" at the OESCA National Independent Specialty over fifteen OES; and Scottbar Kipling, CDX (Susan and Dewey Weiford III), High in Trial (196½) from the Open "B" Class at the OES League of Northern California over nine OES.

Among the CD qualifiers, scores of 195 or better are becoming more common. In 1971, Laca Daisical Daisy, CD, a bitch owned by M. S. Kines, Torrance, California, did it with 198½-197-198. In 1972 the Ken Crumps' Barkaway Ladybird, CD, scored 195-195½-193½ on her way to the degree, and in 1973 the top scores were those of Michael and Joan Wallin's Dusterdown Bear Rug, CD (D), at 195½-196½-197½. By 1975 the ten top-scoring CD titlists among OES were uniformly higher than were their predecessors. It is also interesting to note that in the years prior to 1975 the OES finishing obedience degrees were usually about evenly divided between dogs and bitches, but in 1975 the bitches outnumbered the dogs by two to one and all three of the OES finishing in Utility were bitches.

Only twelve Old English Sheepdogs have earned all three obedience degrees and only one has the current Tracking Dog title, so they are worth mentioning in a little more detail.

The first OES in America to earn all three obedience degrees was Ch. John Marksman, a dog already mentioned in an earlier chapter. Bred and owned by the late Fred LaCrosse, he earned the first degrees in 1942 and the UD in 1946 when he was six years old. He was an outstanding exhibit in conformation rings, as well. He is sometimes listed as having the UDT or UD(T) degree because tracking was required for the UD degree when he was qualified.

The next OES to equal this accomplishment in obedience was a bitch, Driftwood's Little Bo Peep (Driftwood's Billie Barton x Matilda Mia of Driftwood), owned by Anne M. Raker of Lincoln, Massachusetts. She finished the CD in 1961, the CDX in 1962, and her UD in mid-1963 at three years of age. She had two perfect-200 scores in obedience, the only such scores recorded for a Sheepdog, and she won first place in seventeen trials and matches, being three times highest-scoring dog in show. She is recorded by the OESCA as a Register of Merit Dam (1969), having been the dam of at least three champions. She died on June 6, 1970, shortly after her record for earning all three degrees had been equalled by the next triple-degree holder.

Ch. Greyfriar Sir Fang (Greyfriar Fancy Pants x Greyfriar Royal Show-Off) earned his UD degree at nearly six years of age in 1970. Fang is owned by Mrs. Beverly Roupp of Lakewood, Colorado. After he had earned his first "leg" in Utility, the rules and procedures were changed by the AKC so that Fang had to undergo retraining before he could complete the degree, which partly accounts for the fact that he was a little older than perhaps the average when he completed the third obedience degree. He was also trained for the Tracking Dog test as well, but apparently trials for that title are a bit difficult to find at convenient times in some areas.

Three years then passed before the fourth and fifth UD degrees were earned by Bobtails. The fourth UD was earned by Fezziwig Lord Plushbottom (Ch. Fezziwig Ceiling Zero x Cerlyn's Sassie Girl), a dog owned by Mr. and Mrs. Edward Thomson of Cranford, New Jersey, who finished the degree at eight years of age in April of 1973. He also has earned a Canadian CDX degree.

That same year the fifth OES finished the UD degree. Shepton Arrabella (Shepton Benjamin x Shepton Little Pearl), a bitch owned by Dr. and Mrs. Michael Scott of Fair Oaks, California, earned the degree at just under four years of age in August. She finished her CD with an average score of 193½ when she was only eleven months old, and the CDX in only three shows six months later. In the Utility competition she not only qualified for the degree but won First, Second, and Fourth Place with scores of 190-197-188 in large classes.

The sixth UD title was earned in 1974 by Sheplin Raggedyshag (Teddy Bear x Lilly O'Lady), a dog owned by Robert and Deena Mathog of Hopkins, Minnesota. His Utility scores were recorded as 173-186-181 at Minnesota shows in April, May, and July.

In 1975 three more OES bitches completed the UD degree. The

first was Old Weird Wendy II (Carrimount White Prince x Old Weird Wendy), owned by Douglas W. and Sally Heath Lloyd of Melbourne, Florida. Her qualifying scores of 186½-187½-184 were recorded at Florida shows. In 1973 she had been the second highest-scoring Old English Sheepdog in qualifying for her CDX.

Also finishing the UD late in 1975 were Hellzapoppin Nanna (Shaggyboots' Bounce A Bout x Happyshag Lovely Lady), owned by Paul and Loreen Fournier of Oceanside, California, and Miss Nana Pan (Mr. Boo II x Shaggy Nanny), owned by Jean Te Winkel of Minneapolis, Minnesota. Miss Nana Pan scored 191½-191½-188 in Utility and was the highest-scoring OES qualifying for the CDX degree in 1974, with 195½-194-195. Hellzapoppin Nanna scored 185-194-192 in Utility and in 1974 had been the third highest-scoring OES, completing her CDX with 194-190-194½.

In 1976 Blueacre Bonny Blythe (Shepton Blueacre Blue Peter x Little Miss Muffin of Rokeby) owned by Yvette M. and John M. Neary of New Canaan, Connecticut, became the tenth dog on the UD list. Among her scores were 192½ for highest-scoring dog in regular classes at the Old English Sheepdog Club of Greater New York Show in June, 189 at Trumbull, Connecticut, in July, and 190 at Berkley Township, New Jersey, in August.

Smith's Misty Lady owned by Dixie L. Smith became the eleventh OES to win the Utility title late in the summer of 1976, when she recorded scores of 185½-192-173½ at shows in Ohio and Pennsylvania.

The twelfth UD titlist is Scottbar Black Eyed Susan, owned by Richard and Teresa Brandau of McGuire AFB, New Jersey. Her UD scores late in 1976 were 191-177-190 plus 193 and First Place. On September 18, 1977, in her first attempt she earned her Tracking Dog title at the Allentown Dog Training Club trial held in Kutztown, Pennsylvania.

The OES has seldom gone into Tracking Dog competition. There simply isn't that much opportunity to train for the title and to compete. The only other Bobtail recorded as having earned the TD title under the present rules is Silver Snowbear, CD (Ch. Dogpatch's Silver Monarch x Ch. Dogpatch's Monette), owned by M. B. and T. W. Barat, who qualified for the title late in 1968. He had earned his CD degree in May of the same year at shows in the south.

Entry in Tracking Dog competition is not limited to dogs who have qualified for any of the obedience degrees. The TD title may be earned at any time, and trials for it are held apart from dog shows. Only one qualifying score is required for the title.

Ch. Fezziwig Raggedy Andy and a "Fezziwig" granddaughter share "the real thing."

Nap Time. Melinda Jordan resting with furry friend.

The Personality of the Old English Sheepdog

Fifty years ago one writer fittingly described the Old English Sheepdog as follows: "His apparently clumsy action and antics belie his remarkable agility and sagacity, and all in all he is a dog of the highest mentality and a most amusing and companionable pal." The description is equally accurate today.

The Old English Sheepdog is a highly-adaptable dog, being at home (and probably right underfoot) wherever his owner is, indoors or outdoors, no matter the place or climate, so long as he receives the attention to his health and comfort that any such devoted companion deserves. You cannot help giving him the loving he needs, for if you ignore him for long he will remind you of your duty by laying his great big paw gently in your lap and fixing you with that patient, long-suffering look that both adores and forgives you at once.

The Old English Sheepdog is one of the easiest breeds I know of to fit readily into a strange new home or family at any age, and his love of all human beings is such that he adjusts to a new owner with little difficulty. The occasional one, however, is so people-oriented that he does not do well in a boarding kennel, even for a few days, so the conscientious owner who must be absent would do better to hire a "dog sitter" at home.

By nature and despite his size, he is an even-tempered, affectionate, tolerant, and remarkably gentle creature. He is frequently stubborn and persistent, but these are the very characteristics that qualify him as the excellent working dog he has always been. He masquerades as a reliable watchdog (just listen to his bark), but in most circumstances, as a guard of his owner's property he lacks any ultimate authority, unless he should lick an intruder into submission (with his tongue, that is).

The Sheepdog's size will make him a potential liability if he is not trained to restrain his natural tendencies to rough playfulness and effusive demonstrations of friendliness. In fact, given his innate stubbornness, he may not be the easiest dog to train if he

Typical clown. Ch. Pinafore Captain Gruntz, CDX. Owners, Roger and Nancy Smith, Pinafore OES.

Love Machine. Old Sarum's Lord Bumble.

reaches his full size before any consistent training is begun. But even unfettered by civilizing restraints, the delightful personality is captivating. My least-trained and utterly uninhibited one was known by all his friends as "that adorable brat," and he had no enemies.

A natural clown, he loves and delights children. Except for the bumbling exuberance of his early puppyhood, he will be on his most gentle and tolerant behavior with young children, as if to demonstrate his sensitive understanding of what the circumstances require. He will put up with handling by children that he might never tolerate from their elders, and stories of toddlers who learned to walk by hanging onto the Sheepdog's coat as he led them carefully about the room are typical of his forebearance.

One of mine would tackle a teenager like a linebacker in the yard, but would quietly approach a baby in a stroller and calmly wait for the baby to reach out to him.

About the only working assignment to which the Old English Sheepdog is patently not very well adapted is that of a seeing-eye dog, but I expect he could serve well in even that capacity if asked. While he was traditionally bred and used as a drover's dog (his instinct for that has been called "ineradicable"), he has been successfully employed in any number of other jobs from sheep-herding to hunting and retrieving. During World War II an Old English Sheepdog owned by Donald Davidson of Akron, Ohio, was even clipped short and enlisted in the K-9 Corps for guard duty.

Such a dog must obviously, then, be notable for his intelligence, and Aubrey Hopwood, one of the best-known English breeders and writers on the breed, acknowledged that "every authority is unanimous in ascribing to him exceptional sagacity."[1]

Even if you don't happen to come across a utilitarian Sheepdog today, in simply living with one of them you must be impressed with his intelligence. Dumb he may be (no human speech, that is), but he talks to you; and if you are clever enough, you will understand him. From experience, I am convinced that as a member of your family, it is *he* who trains *you*. The habit and routine into which your life together falls is likely to be *his* habit and *his* routine, though being an intelligent creature, he will readily compromise any issue when you insist.

Ask any Sheepdog owner and he will give you an apparently endless number of anecdotes, all attesting to the extraordinary sensitivity and reasoning intelligence of the breed. One such story, for

1. Aubrey Hopwood, *The Old English Sheepdog (From Puppyhood to Champion)*, Bickers, London, 1905.

The OES is a good breed for children in Junior Showmanship. Thirteen-month-old "Ralph" with Junior Handler Jeannine Boyer, 1967. Note more natural shaggy ring appearance of those days. This is the immature light gray stage. Photo by The Lawrence, Kansas, *Journal-World*.

Puppy curiosity. Tamara's Peaches and Cream (six months) with her downy friends. Tamara Kennels, Brighton, Michigan.

example, tells of how an aging Sheepdog, blind and becoming feeble, was for all of his last years gently urged to exercise, guided about, herded around corners, constantly accompanied, and rescued from danger by another Sheepdog, a son of the old one, who had appointed himself to the task.[2]

The Old English Sheepdog can be a master of calculated comedy. Watch these characters in the obedience ring! They are natural-born "hams" who play to the audience, and they know better than we do how essentially ridiculous it is to aim for some sort of artificial precision in performing a dull routine when they can create interest and variety in it for us.

Once I saw a Sheepdog of my acquaintance sent (under the older rules) to seek the dropped glove in the Utility Class. At the first corner on his way, he chanced to come upon a friend of the same breed who was just outside the ring waiting to enter a conformation class in the adjoining ring. Naturally, being a friendly fellow above all else, he paused to say hello and pass the time of day with his friend. What with this and that, he forgot the purpose of his trip and finally sat down to consider his situation. With the realization of what he had done, he took on such a foolish expression of chagrin and embarrassment that even the judge had to laugh outright. The spectators were with him all the way (and don't think he didn't know it), but the judge, though entertained, was not moved to mercy.

Perhaps the Sheepdog's basic nature has been expressed best by Dame Ethel Smyth, British composer and conductor, whose book about her succession of Old English Sheepdogs, *Inordinate (?) Affection*, was published privately in England about 1936.

Dame Ethel had received her first Sheepdog from a friend in 1899 who told her, "Once you've had one of these, no other sort of dog will do you." She found the prediction accurate, and she wrote: "I called him and all his successors 'Pan' because there is something in the shaggy appearance of this race, their wistful human eyes, their deprecating gentleness alternating with the wildest of spirits, that suggests primitive ages when nymphs, fauns, and satyrs were an orthodox part of the scheme and associated on equal terms with human beings."

2. W. Graham Robertson, *Life Was Worth Living*, Harper & Brothers, New York and London, 1931.

Puppies are always curious. Some plants are poisonous to animals. Protect your puppies from dangerous plants.

"Shaggy Boy" and his playthings. Surprisingly, the Sheepdog does not often destroy his stuffed toys but "mothers" them.

Daisy and family at the Grand Canyon. Sheepdogs are welcome everywhere.

Manners for the Family Dog

Although each dog has personality quirks and idiosyncrasies that set him apart as an individual, dogs in general have two characteristics that can be utilized to advantage in training. The first is the dog's strong desire to please, which has been built up through centuries of association with man. The second lies in the innate quality of the dog's mentality. It has been proved conclusively that while dogs have reasoning power, their learning ability is based on a direct association of cause and effect, so that they willingly repeat acts that bring pleasant results and discontinue acts that bring unpleasant results. Hence, to take fullest advantage of a dog's abilities, the trainer must make sure the dog understands a command, and then reward him when he obeys and correct him when he does wrong.

Commands should be as short as possible and should be repeated in the same way, day after day. Saying "Heel," one day, and "Come here and heel," the next will confuse the dog. *Heel, sit, stand, stay, down,* and *come* are standard terminology, and are preferable for a dog that may later be given advanced training.

Tone of voice is important, too. For instance, a coaxing tone helps cajole a young puppy into trying something new. Once an exercise is mastered, commands given in a firm, matter-of-fact voice give the dog confidence in his own ability. Praise, expressed in an exuberant tone, will tell the dog quite clearly that he has earned his master's approval. On the other hand, a firm "No" indicates with equal clarity that he has done wrong.

Rewards for good performance may consist simply of praising lavishly and petting the dog, although many professional trainers use bits of food as rewards. Tidbits are effective only if the dog is hungry, of course. And if you smoke, you must be sure to wash your hands before each training session, for the odor of nicotine is repulsive to dogs. On the hands of a heavy smoker, the odor of nicotine may be so strong that the dog is unable to smell the tidbit.

Correction for wrong-doing should be limited to repeating "No," in a scolding tone of voice or to confining the dog to his bed. Spanking or striking the dog is taboo—particularly using sticks, which might cause injury, but the hand should never be used either. For field training as well as some obedience work, the hand is used to signal the dog. Dogs that have been punished by slapping have a tendency to cringe whenever they see a hand raised and consequently do not respond promptly when the owner's intent is not to punish but to signal.

Some trainers recommend correcting the dog by whacking him with a rolled-up newspaper. The idea is that the newspaper will not injure the dog but that the resulting noise will condition the dog to avoid repeating the act that seemingly caused the noise. Many authorities object to this type of correction, for it may result in the dog's becoming "noise-shy"—a decided disadvantage with show dogs which must maintain poise in adverse, often noisy, situations. "Noise-shyness" is also an unfortunate reaction in field dogs, since it may lead to gun-shyness.

To be effective, correction must be administered immediately, so that in the dog's mind there is a direct connection between his act and the correction. You can make voice corrections under almost any circumstances, but you must never call the dog to you and then correct him, or he will associate the correction with the fact that he has come and will become reluctant to respond. If the dog is at a distance and doing something he shouldn't, go to him and scold him while he is still involved in wrong-doing. If this is impossible, ignore the offense until he repeats it. Then correct him properly.

Especially while a dog is young, he should be watched closely and stopped before he gets into mischief. All dogs need to do a certain amount of chewing, so to prevent your puppy's chewing something you value, provide him with his own balls and toys. Never allow him to chew cast-off slippers and then expect him to differentiate between cast-off items and those you value. Nylon stockings, wooden articles, and various other items may cause intestinal obstructions if the dog chews and swallows them, and death may result. Rubber and plastic toys may also be harmful if they are of types the dog can bite through or chew into pieces and then swallow. So it is essential that the dog be permitted to chew only on bones or toys he cannot chew up and swallow.

Serious training for obedience should not be started until a dog is a year old. But basic training in house manners should begin the day the puppy enters his new home. A puppy should never be given the run of the house but should be confined to a box or small pen except for play periods when you can devote full attention to him. The first thing to teach the dog is his name, so that whenever he hears it, he will immediately come to attention. Whenever you are near his box, talk to him, using his name repeatedly. During play periods, talk to him, pet him, and handle him, for he must be conditioned so he will not object to being handled by a veterinarian, show judge, or family friend. As the dog investigates his surroundings, watch him carefully and if he tries something he shouldn't, reprimand him with a scolding "No!" If he repeats the offense, scold him and confine him to his box, then praise him. Discipline must be prompt, consistent, and always followed with praise. Never tease the dog, and never allow others to do so. Kindness and understanding are essential to a pleasant, mutually rewarding relationship.

When the puppy is two to three months old, secure a flat, narrow leather collar and have him start wearing it (never use a harness, which will encourage tugging and pulling). After a week or so, attach a light leather lead to the collar during play sessions and let the puppy walk around, dragging the lead behind him. Then start holding the end of the lead and coaxing the puppy to come to you. He will then be fully accustomed to collar and lead when you start taking him outside while he is being housebroken.

Housebreaking can be accomplished in a matter of approximately two weeks provided you wait until the dog is mature enough to have some control over bodily functions. This is usually at about four months. Until that time, the puppy should spend most of his day confined to his penned area, with the floor covered with several thicknesses of newspapers so that he may relieve himself when necessary without damage to floors.

Either of two methods works well in housebreaking—the choice depending upon where you live. If you live in a house with a readily accessible yard, you will probably want to train the puppy from the beginning to go outdoors. If you live in an apartment without easy access to a yard, you may decide to train him first to relieve himself on newspapers and then when he has learned control, to teach the puppy to go outdoors.

If you decide to train the puppy by taking him outdoors, arrange some means of confining him indoors where you can watch him closely—in a small penned area, or tied to a short lead (five or six feet). Dogs are naturally clean animals, reluctant to soil their quarters, and confining the puppy to a limited area will encourage him to avoid making a mess.

A young puppy must be taken out often, so watch your puppy closely and if he indicates he is about to relieve himself, take him out at once. If he has an accident, scold him and take him out so he will associate the act of going outside with the need to relieve himself. Always take the puppy out within an hour after meals—preferably to the same place each time—and make sure he relieves himself before you return him to the house. Restrict his water for two hours before bedtime and take him out just before you retire for the night. When you wake in the morning, take him out again.

For paper training, set aside a particular room and cover a large area of the floor with several thicknesses of newspapers. Confine the dog on a short leash and each time he relieves himself, remove the soiled papers and replace them with clean ones.

As his control increases, gradually decrease the paper area, leaving part of the floor bare. If he uses the bare floor, scold him mildly and put him on the papers, letting him know that there is where he is to relieve himself. As he comes to understand the idea, increase the bare area until papers cover only space equal to approximately two full newspaper sheets. Keep him using the papers, but begin taking him out on a leash at the times of day that he habitually relieves himself. Watch him closely when he is indoors and at the first sign that he needs to go, take him outdoors. With this method too, restrict the puppy's water for two hours before bedtime, but if necessary, permit him to use the papers before you retire for the night.

Using either method, the puppy will be housebroken in an amazingly short time. Once he has learned control he will need to relieve himself only four or five times a day.

Informal obedience training, started at the age of about six to eight months, will provide a good background for any advanced training you may decide to give your dog later. The collar most effective for training is the metal chain-link variety. The correct size for your dog will be about one inch longer than the measurement around the largest part of his head. The chain must be slipped through one of the rings so the collar forms a loop. The collar should be put on with the loose ring at the right of the dog's neck, the chain attached to it coming over the neck and through the holding ring, rather than under the neck. Since the dog is to be at your left for most of the training, this makes the collar most effective.

The leash should be attached to the loose ring, and should be either webbing or leather, six feet long and a half inch to a full inch

Chain-link collar. The collar should be removed whenever the dog is not under your immediate supervision, for many dogs have met death by strangulation when a collar was left on and became entangled in some object.

wide. When you want your dog's attention, or wish to correct him, give a light, quick pull on the leash, which will momentarily tighten the collar about the neck. Release the pressure instantly, and the correction will have been made. If the puppy is already accustomed to a leather collar, he will adjust easily to the training collar. But before you start training sessions, practice walking with the dog until he responds readily when you increase tension on the leash.

Set aside a period of fifteen minutes, once or twice a day, for regular training sessions, and train in a place where there will be no distractions. Teach only one exercise at a time, making sure the dog has mastered it before going on to another. It will probably take at least a week for the dog to master each exercise. As training progresses, start each session by reviewing exercises the dog has already learned, then go on to the new exercise for a period of concerted practice. When discipline is required, make the correction immediately, and always praise the dog after corrections as well as when he obeys promptly. During each session stick strictly to business. Afterwards, take time to play with the dog.

The first exercise to teach is heeling. Have the dog at your left and hold the leash as shown in the illustration on the preceding page. Start walking, and just as you put your foot forward for the first step, say your dog's name to get his attention, followed by the command, "Heel!" Simultaneously, pull on the leash lightly. As you walk, try to keep the dog at your left side, with his head alongside your left leg. Pull on the leash as necessary to urge him forward or back, to right or left, but keep him in position. Each time you pull on the leash, say "Heel!" and praise the dog lavishly. When the dog heels properly in a straight line, start making circles, turning corners, etc.

Once the dog has learned to heel well, start teaching the "sit." Each time you stop while heeling, command "Sit!" The dog will be at your left, so use your left hand to press on his rear and guide him to a sitting position, while you use the leash in your right hand to keep his head up. Hold him in position for a few moments while you praise him, then give the command to heel. Walk a few steps, stop, and repeat the procedure. Before long he will automatically sit whenever you stop. You can then teach the dog to "sit" from any position.

When the dog will sit on command without correction, he is ready to learn to stay until you release him. Simply sit him, command "Stay!" and hold him in position for perhaps half a minute, repeating "Stay," if he attempts to stand. You can release him by saying "O.K." Gradually increase the time until he will stay on command for three or four minutes.

The "stand-stay" should also be taught when the dog is on leash. While you are heeling, stop and give the command "Stand!" Keep the dog from sitting by quickly placing your left arm under him, immediately in front of his right hind leg. If he continues to try to sit, don't scold him but start up again with the heel command, walk a few steps, and stop again, repeating the stand command and preventing the dog from sitting. Once the dog has mastered the stand, teach him to stay by holding him in position and repeating the word "Stay!"

The "down stay" will prove beneficial in many situations, but especially if you wish to take your dog in the car without confining him to a crate. To teach the "down," have the dog sitting at your side with collar and leash on. If he is a large dog, step forward with the leash in your hand and turn so you face him. Let the leash touch the floor, then step over it with your right foot so it is under the instep of your shoe. Grasping the leash low down with both hands, slowly pull up, saying, "Down!" Hold the leash taut until the dog goes down. Once he responds well, teach the dog to stay in the down position (the down-stay), using the same method as for the sit- and stand-stays.

To teach small dogs the "down," another method may be used. Have the dog sit at your side, then kneel beside him. Reach across his back with your left arm, and take hold of his left front leg close to the body. At the same time, with your right hand take hold of his right front leg close to his body. As you command "Down!" gently lift the legs and place the dog in the down position. Release your hold on his legs and slide your left hand onto his back, repeating, "Down, stay," while keeping him in position.

The "come" is taught when the dog is on leash and heeling. Simply walk along, then suddenly take a step backward, saying "Come!" Pull the leash as you give the command and the dog will turn and follow you. Continue walking backward, repeatedly saying "Come," and tightening the leash if necessary.

Once the dog has mastered the exercises while on leash, try taking the leash off and going through the same routine, beginning with the heeling exercise. If the dog doesn't respond promptly, he needs review with the leash on. But patience and persistence will be rewarded, for you will have a dog you can trust to respond promptly under all conditions.

Even after they are well trained, dogs sometimes develop bad habits that are hard to break. Jumping on people is a common habit, and all members of the family must assist if it is to be broken. If the dog is a large or medium breed, take a step forward and raise your knee just as he starts to jump on you. As your knee strikes the dog's chest, command "Down!" in a scolding voice. When a small dog jumps on you, take both front paws in your hands, and, while talking in a pleasant tone of voice, step on the dog's back feet just hard enough to hurt them slightly. With either method the dog is taken by surprise and doesn't associate the discomfort with the person causing it.

Occasionally a dog may be too chummy with guests who don't care for dogs. If the dog has had obedience training, simply command "Come!" When he responds, have him sit beside you.

Excessive barking is likely to bring complaints from neighbors, and persistent efforts may be needed to subdue a dog that barks without provocation. To correct the habit, you must be close to the dog when he starts barking. Encircle his muzzle with both hands, hold his mouth shut, and command "Quiet!" in a firm voice. He should soon learn to respond so you can control him simply by giving the command.

Sniffing other dogs is an annoying habit. If the dog is off leash and sniffs other dogs, ignoring your commands to come, he needs

Benching area at Westminster Kennel Club Show.

to review the lessons on basic behavior. When the dog is on leash, scold him, then pull on the leash, command "Heel," and walk away from the other dog.

A well-trained dog will be no problem if you decide to take him with you when you travel. No matter how well he responds, however, he should never be permitted off leash when you walk him in a strange area. Distractions will be more tempting, and there will be more chance of his being attacked by other dogs. So whenever the dog travels with you, take his leash along—and use it.

Judging for Best in Show at Westminster Kennel Club Show.

Show Competition

Centuries ago, it was common practice to hold agricultural fairs in conjunction with spring and fall religious festivals, and to these gatherings, cattle, dogs, and other livestock were brought for exchange. As time went on, it became customary to provide entertainment, too. Dogs often participated in such sporting events as bull baiting, bear baiting, and ratting. Then the dog that exhibited the greatest skill in the arena was also the one that brought the highest price when time came for barter or sale. Today, these fairs seem a far cry from our highly organized bench shows and field trials. But they were the forerunners of modern dog shows and played an important role in shaping the development of purebred dogs.

The first organized dog show was held at Newcastle, England, in 1859. Later that same year, a show was held at Birmingham. At both shows dogs were divided into four classes and only Pointers and Setters were entered. In 1860, the first dog show in Germany was held at Apoldo, where nearly one hundred dogs were exhibited and entries were divided into six groups. Interest expanded rapidly, and by the time the Paris Exhibition was held in 1878, the dog show was a fixture of international importance.

In the United States, the first organized bench show was held in 1874 in conjunction with the meeting of the Illinois State Sportsmen's Association in Chicago, and all entries were dogs of sporting breeds. Although the show was a rather casual affair, interest spread quickly. Before the end of the year, shows were held in Oswego, New York, Mineola, Long Island, and Memphis, Tennessee. And the latter combined a bench show with the first organized field trial ever held in the United States. In January 1875, an all-breed show (the first in the United States) was held at Detroit, Michigan. From then on, interest increased rapidly, though rules were not always uniform, for there was no organization through which to coordinate activities until September 1884 when The American Kennel Club was founded. Now the largest dog registering organization in the world, the AKC is an association of several hundred member clubs—all breed, specialty, field trial, and obedience groups—each represented by a delegate to the AKC.

The several thousand shows and trials held annually in the United States do much to stimulate interest in breeding to produce better looking, sounder, purebred dogs. For breeders, shows provide a means of measuring the merits of their work as compared with accomplishments of other breeders. For hundreds of thousands of dog fanciers, they provide an absorbing hobby.

Bench Shows

At bench (or conformation) shows, dogs are rated comparatively on their physical qualities (or conformation) in accordance with breed Standards which have been approved by The American Kennel Club. Characteristics such as size, coat, color, placement of eye or ear, general soundness, etc., are the basis for selecting the best dog in a class. Only purebred dogs are eligible to compete and if the show is one where points toward a championship are to be awarded, a dog must be at least six months old.

Bench shows are of various types. An all-breed show has classes for all of the breeds recognized by The American Kennel Club as well as a Miscellaneous Class for breeds not recognized, such as the Australian Cattle Dog, the Ibizan Hound, the Spinoni Italiani, etc. A sanctioned match is an informal meeting where dogs compete but not for championship points. A specialty show is confined to a single breed. Other shows may restrict entries to champions of record, to American-bred dogs, etc. Competition for Junior Showmanship or for Best Brace, Best Team, or Best Local Dog may be included. Also, obedience competition is held in conjunction with many bench shows.

The term "bench show" is somewhat confusing in that shows of this type may be either "benched" or "unbenched." At the former, each dog is assigned an individual numbered stall where he must remain throughout the show except for times when he is being judged, groomed, or exercised. At unbenched shows, no stalls are provided and dogs are kept in their owners' cars or in crates when not being judged.

A show where a dog is judged for conformation actually constitutes an elimination contest. To begin with, the dogs of a single breed compete with others of their breed in one of the regular classes: Puppy, Novice, Bred by Exhibitor, American-Bred, or

Open, and, finally, Winners, where the top dogs of the preceding five classes meet. The next step is the judging for Best of Breed (or Best of Variety of Breed). Here the Winners Dog and Winners Bitch (or the dog named Winners if only one prize is awarded) compete with any champions that are entered, together with any undefeated dogs that have competed in additional non-regular classes. The dog named Best of Breed (or Best of Variety of Breed), then goes on to compete with the other Best of Breed winners in his Group. The dogs that win in Group competition then compete for the final and highest honor, Best in Show.

When the Winners Class is divided by sex, championship points are awarded the Winners Dog and Winners Bitch. If the Winners Class is not divided by sex, championship points are awarded the dog or bitch named Winners. The number of points awarded varies, depending upon such factors as the number of dogs competing, the Schedule of Points established by the Board of Directors of the AKC, and whether the dog goes on to win Best of Breed, the Group, and Best in Show.

In order to become a champion, a dog must win fifteen points, including points from at least two major wins—that is, at least two shows where three or more points are awarded. The major wins must be under two different judges, and one or more of the remaining points must be won under a third judge. The most points ever awarded at a show is five and the least is one, so, in order to become a champion, a dog must be exhibited and win in at least three shows, and usually he is shown many times before he wins his championship.

Pure Bred Dogs—American Kennel Gazette and other dog magazines contain lists of forthcoming shows, together with names and addresses of sponsoring organizations to which you may write for entry forms and information relative to fees, closing dates, etc. Before entering your dog in a show for the first time, you should familiarize yourself with the regulations and rules governing competition. You may secure such information from The American Kennel Club or from a local dog club specializing in your breed. It is essential that you also familiarize yourself with the AKC approved Standard for your breed so you will be fully aware of characteristics worthy of merit as well as those considered faulty, or possibly even serious enough to disqualify the dog from competition. For instance, monorchidism (failure of one testicle to descend) and cryptorchidism (failure of both testicles to descend) are disqualifying faults in all breeds.

If possible, you should first attend a show as a spectator and observe judging procedures from ringside. It will also be helpful to join a local breed club and to participate in sanctioned matches before entering an all-breed show.

The dog should be equipped with a narrow leather show lead and a show collar—never an ornamented or spiked collar. For benched shows, either a bench crate or a metal-link bench chain to fasten the dog to the bench will be needed. For unbenched shows, the dog's crate should be taken along so that he may be confined in comfort when he is not appearing in the ring. A dog should never be left in a car with all the windows closed. In hot weather the temperature will become unbearable in a very short time. Heat exhaustion may result from even a short period of confinement, and death may ensue.

Food and water dishes will be needed, as well as a supply of the food and water to which the dog is accustomed. Brushes and combs are also necessary, so that you may give the dog's coat a final grooming after you arrive at the show.

Familiarize yourself with the schedule of classes ahead of time, for the dog must be fed and exercised and permitted to relieve himself, and any last-minute grooming completed before his class is called. Both you and the dog should be ready to enter the ring unhurriedly. A good deal of skill in conditioning, training, and handling is required if a dog is to be presented properly. And it is essential that the handler himself be composed, for a jittery handler will transmit his nervousness to his dog.

Once the class is assembled in the ring, the judge will ask that the dogs be paraded in line, moving counter-clockwise in a circle. If you have trained your dog well, you will have no difficulty controlling him in the ring, where he must change pace quickly and gracefully and walk and trot elegantly and proudly with head erect. The show dog must also stand quietly for inspection, posing like a statue for several minutes while the judge observes his structure in detail, examines teeth, feet, coat, etc. When the judge calls your dog forward for individual inspection, do not attempt to converse, but answer any questions he may ask.

As the judge examines the class, he measures each dog against the ideal described in the Standard, then measures the dogs against each other in a comparative sense and selects for first place the dog that comes closest to conforming to the Standard for its breed. If your dog isn't among the winners, don't grumble. If he places first, don't brag loudly. For a bad loser is disgusting, but a poor winner is insufferable.

Junior Showmanship Competition at Westminster Kennel Club Show.

Bench crate.

Wagon crate.

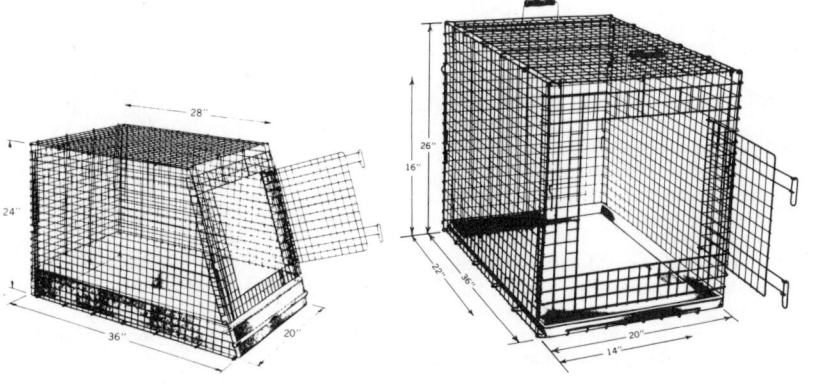

Collars. At the top are two "pinch" or "spiked" collars that are not permitted in AKC shows. Below are two permissible "choke" collars, the one on the right of steel chain and the one on the left of braided nylon. While the choke collars are permitted in conformation shows, they are used more often in obedience competition.

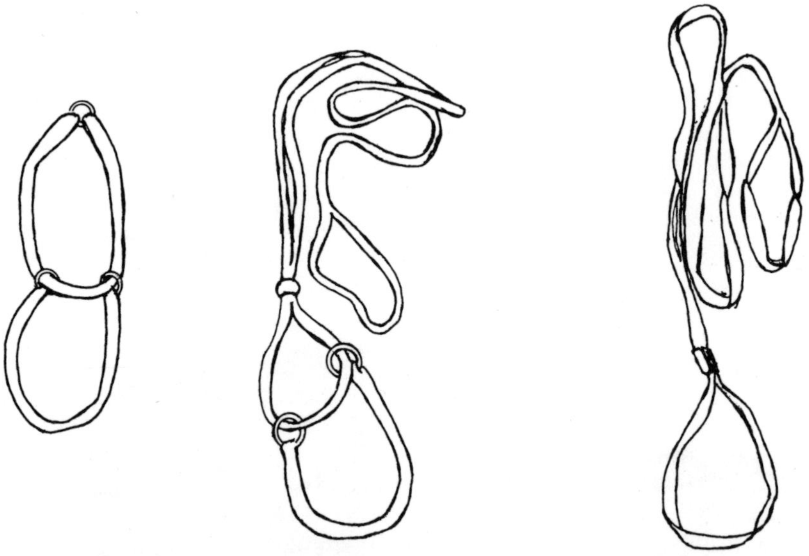

Left, "English" or "Martingale" collar to which lead would be attached. Center, "English" or "Martingale" collar and lead. In using either of these, the dog's head would be inserted through the lower loop. Right, nylon slip lead. Collars and leads of these three types are preferred for conformation showing because they give better control for stacking a dog than the "choke" collars.

Obedience Competition

For hundreds of years, dogs have been used in England and Germany in connection with police and guard work, and their working potential has been evaluated through tests devised to show agility, strength, and courage. Organized training has also been popular with English and German breeders for many years, although it was first practiced primarily for the purpose of training large breeds in aggressive tactics.

There was little interest in obedience training in the United States until 1933 when Mrs. Whitehouse Walker returned from England and enthusiastically introduced the sport. Two years later, Mrs. Walker persuaded The American Kennel Club to approve organized obedience activities and to assume jurisdiction over obedience rules. Since then, interest has increased at a phenomenal rate, for obedience competition is not only a sport the average spectator can follow readily, but also a sport for which the average owner can train his own dog easily. Obedience competition is suitable for all breeds. Furthermore, there is no limit to the number of dogs that may win in competition, for each dog is scored individually on the basis of a point rating system.

The dog is judged on his response to certain commands, and if he gains a high enough score in three successive trials under different judges, he wins an obedience degree. Degrees awarded are "CD"—Companion Dog; "CDX"—Companion Dog Excellent; and "UD"—Utility Dog. A fourth degree, the "TD" or Tracking Dog degree, may be won at any time and tests for it are held apart from dog shows. The qualifying score is a minimum of 170 points out of a possible total of 200, with no score in any one exercise less than 50% of the points allotted.

Since obedience titles are progressive, earlier titles (with the exception of the tracking degree) are dropped as a dog acquires the next higher degree. If an obedience title is gained in another country in addition to the United States, that fact is signified by the word "International," followed by the title.

Trials for obedience trained dogs are held at most of the larger bench shows, and obedience training clubs are to be found in almost all communities today. Information concerning forthcoming trials and lists of obedience training clubs are included regularly in *Pure Bred Dogs–American Kennel Gazette*—and other dog magazines. Pamphlets containing rules and regulations governing obedience competition are available upon request from The American Kennel Club, 51 Madison Avenue, New York, N.Y. 10010. Rules are revised occasionally, so if you are interested in participating in obedience competition, you should be sure your copy of the regulations is current.

All dogs must comply with the same rules, although in broad jump, high jump, and bar jump competition, the jumps are adjusted to the size of the breed. Classes at obedience trials are divided into Novice (A and B), Open (A and B), and Utility (which may be divided into A and B, at the option of the sponsoring club and with the approval of The American Kennel Club).

The Novice class is for dogs that have not won the title Companion Dog. In Novice A, no person who has previously handled a dog that has won a CD title in the obedience ring at a licensed or member trial, and no person who has regularly trained such a dog, may enter or handle a dog. The handler must be the dog's owner or a member of the owner's immediate family. In Novice B, dogs may be handled by the owner or any other person.

The Open A class is for dogs that have won the CD title but have not won the CDX title. Obedience judges and licensed handlers may not enter or handle dogs in this class. Each dog must be handled by the owner or by a member of his immediate family. The Open B class is for dogs that have won the title CD or CDX. A dog may continue to compete in this class after it has won the title UD. Dogs in this class may be handled by the owner or any other person.

The Utility class is for dogs that have won the title CDX. Dogs that have won the title UD may continue to compete in this class, and dogs may be handled by the owner or any other person. Provided the AKC approves, a club may choose to divide the Utility class into Utility A and Utility B. When this is done, the Utility A class is for dogs that have won the title CDX and have not won the title UD. Obedience judges and licensed handlers may not enter or handle dogs in this class. All other dogs that are eligible for the Utility class but not eligible for Utility A may be entered in Utility B.

Novice competition includes such exercises as heeling on and off lead, the stand for examination, coming on recall, and the long sit and the long down.

In Open competition, the dog must perform such exercises as heeling free, the drop on recall, and the retrieve on the flat and over the high jump. Also, he must execute the broad jump, and the long sit and long down.

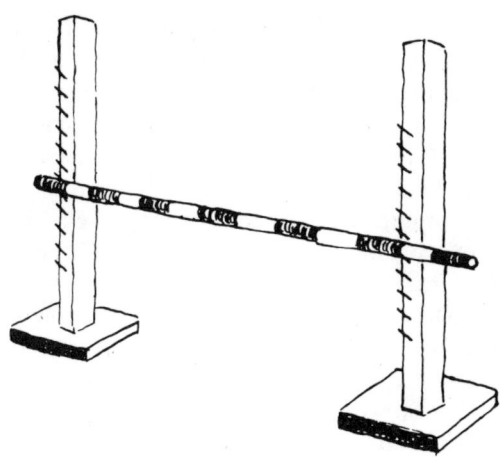

Bar Jump.

In the Utility class, competition includes scent discrimination, the directed retrieve, the signal exercise, directed jumping, and the group examination.

Tracking is the most difficult test. It is always done out-of-doors, of course, and, for obvious reasons, cannot be held at a dog show. The dog must follow a scent trail that is about a quarter mile in length. He is also required to find a scent object (glove, wallet, or other article) left by a stranger who has walked the course to lay down the scent. The dog is required to follow the trail a half to two hours after the scent is laid.

An ideal way to train a dog for obedience competition is to join an obedience class or a training club. In organized class work, beginners' classes cover pretty much the same exercises as those described in the chapter on manners. However, through class work you will develop greater precision than is possible in training your dog by yourself. Amateur handlers often cause the dog to be penalized, for if the handler fails to abide by the rules, it is the dog that suffers the penalty. A common infraction of the rules is using more than one signal or command where regulations stipulate only one may be used. Classwork will help eliminate such errors, which the owner may make unconsciously if he is working alone. Working with a class will also acquaint both dog and handler with ring procedure so that obedience trials will not present unforeseen problems.

Thirty or forty owners and dogs often comprise a class, and exercises are performed in unison, with individual instruction provided if it is required. The procedure followed in training—in fact, even wording of various commands—may vary from instructor to instructor. Equipment used will vary somewhat, also, but will usually include a training collar and leash, a long line, a dumbbell, and a jumping stick. The latter may be a short length of heavy doweling or a broom handle and both it and the dumbbell are usually painted white for increased visibility.

A bitch in season must never be taken to a training class, so before enrolling a female dog, you should determine whether she may be expected to come into season before classes are scheduled to end. If you think she will, it is better to wait and enroll her in a later course, rather than start the course and then miss classes for several weeks.

In addition to the time devoted to actual work in class, the dog must have regular, daily training sessions for practice at home. Before each class or home training session, the dog should be exercised so he will not be highly excited when the session starts, and he must be given an opportunity to relieve himself before the session begins. (Should he have an accident during the class, it is your responsibility to clean up after him.) The dog should be fed several hours before time for the class to begin or else after the class is over—never just before going to class.

If you decide to enter your dog in obedience competition, it is well to enter a small, informal show the first time. Dogs are usually called in the order in which their names appear in the catalog, so as soon as you arrive at the show, acquaint yourself with the schedule. If your dog is not the first to be judged, spend some time at ringside, observing the routine so you will know what to expect when your dog's turn comes.

In addition to collar, leash, and other equipment, you should take your dog's food and water pans and a supply of the food and water to which he is accustomed. You should also take his brushes and combs in order to give him a last-minute brushing before you enter the ring. It is important that the dog look his best even though he isn't to be judged on his appearance.

Before entering the ring, exercise your dog, give him a drink of water, and permit him to relieve himself. Once your dog enters the ring, give him your full attention and be sure to give voice commands distinctly so he will hear and understand, for there will be many distractions at ringside.

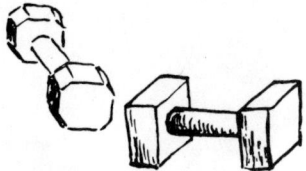

Dumbbells.

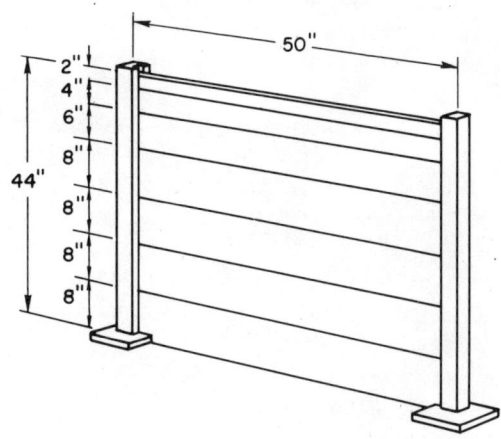

Solid hurdle.

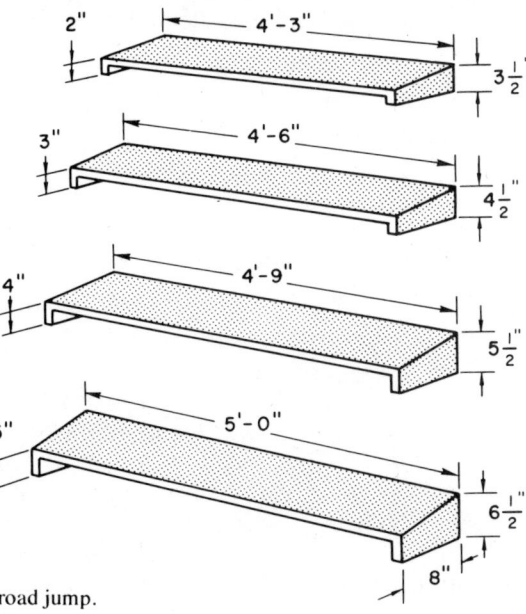

Broad jump.

Top dogs in Utility Class. This illustrates the variety of breeds that compete in obedience.

Genetics

Genetics, the science of heredity, deals with the processes by which physical and mental traits of parents are transmitted to offspring. For centuries, man has been trying to solve these puzzles, but only in the last two hundred years has significant progress been made.

During the eighteenth century, Kölreuter, a German scientist, made revolutionary discoveries concerning plant sexuality and hybridization but was unable to explain just how hereditary processes worked. In the middle of the nineteenth century, Gregor Johann Mendel, an Augustinian monk, experimented with the ordinary garden pea and made other discoveries of major significance. He found that an inherited characteristic was inherited as a complete unit, and that certain characteristics predominated over others. Next, he observed that the hereditary characteristics of each parent are contained in each offspring, even when they are not visible, and that "hidden" characteristics can be transferred without change in their nature to the grandchildren, or even later generations. Finally, he concluded that although heredity contains an element of uncertainty, some things are predictable on the basis of well-defined mathematical laws.

Unfortunately, Mendel's published paper went unheeded, and when he died in 1884 he was still virtually unknown to the scientific world. But other researchers were making discoveries, too. In 1900, three different scientists reported to learned societies that much of their research in hereditary principles had been proved years before by Gregor Mendel and that findings matched perfectly.

Thus, hereditary traits were proved to be transmitted through the chromosomes found in pairs in every living being, one of each pair contributed by the mother, the other by the father. Within each chromosome have been found hundreds of smaller structures, or genes, which are the actual determinants of hereditary characteristics. Some genes are dominant and will be seen in the offspring. Others are recessive and will not be outwardly apparent, yet can be passed on to the offspring to combine with a similar recessive gene of the other parent and thus be seen. Or they may be passed on to the offspring, not be outwardly apparent, but be passed on again to become apparent in a later generation.

Once the genetic theory of inheritance became widely known, scientists began drawing a well-defined line between inheritance and environment. More recent studies show some overlapping of these influences and indicate a combination of the two may be responsible for certain characteristics. For instance, studies have proved that extreme cold increases the amount of black pigment in the skin and hair of the "Himalayan" rabbit, although it has little or no effect on the white or colored rabbit. Current research also indicates that even though characteristics are determined by the genes, some environmental stress occurring at a particular period of pregnancy might cause physical change in the embryo.

Long before breeders had any knowledge of genetics, they practiced one of its most important principles—selective breeding. Experience quickly showed that "like begets like," and by breeding like with like and discarding unlike offspring, the various individual breeds were developed to the point where variations were relatively few. Selective breeding is based on the idea of maintaining the quality of a breed at the highest possible level, while improving whatever defects are prevalent. It requires that only the top dogs in a litter be kept for later breeding, and that inferior specimens be ruthlessly eliminated.

In planning any breeding program, the first requisite is a definite goal—that is, to have clearly in mind a definite picture of the type of dog you wish eventually to produce. To attempt to breed perfection is to approach the problem unrealistically. But if you don't breed for improvement, it is preferable that you not breed at all.

As a first step, you should select a bitch that exemplifies as many of the desired characteristics as possible and mate her with a dog that also has as many of the desired characteristics as possible. If you start with mediocre pets, you will produce mediocre pet puppies. If you decide to start with more than one bitch, all should closely approach the type you desire, since you will then stand a better chance of producing uniformly good puppies from all. Breeders often start with a single bitch and keep the best bitches in every succeeding generation.

Experienced breeders look for "prepotency" in breeding stock—that is, the ability of a dog or bitch to transmit traits to most or all of its offspring. While the term is usually used to describe the transmission of good qualities, a dog may also be prepotent in

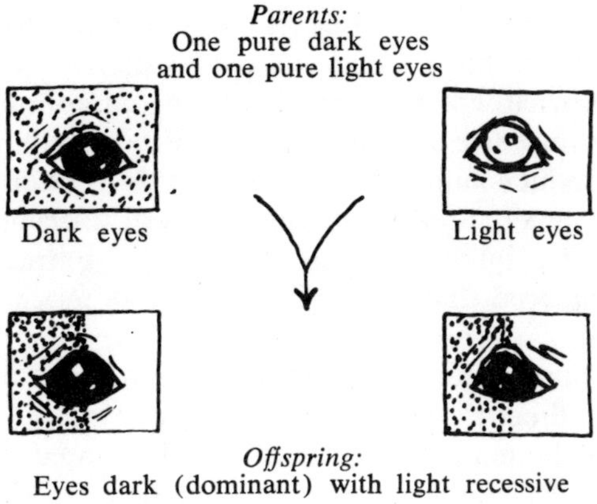

Parents:
One pure dark eyes
and one pure light eyes

Dark eyes　　　　　　　　Light eyes

Offspring:
Eyes dark (dominant) with light recessive

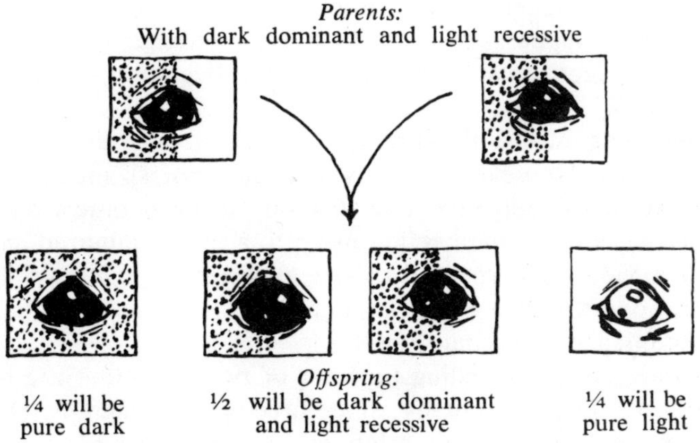

Parents:
With dark dominant and light recessive

Offspring:

¼ will be
pure dark

½ will be dark dominant
and light recessive

¼ will be
pure light

The above is a schematic representation of the Mendelian law as it applies to the inheritance of eye color. The law applies in the same way to the inheritance of other physical characteristics.

transmitting faults. To be prepotent in a practical sense, a dog must possess many characteristics controlled by dominant genes. If desired characteristics are recessive, they will be apparent in the offspring only if carried by both sire and dam. Prepotent dogs and bitches usually come from a line of prepotent ancestors, but the mere fact that a dog has exceptional ancestors will not necessarily mean that he himself will produce exceptional offspring.

A single dog may sire a tremendous number of puppies, whereas a bitch can produce only a comparatively few litters during her lifetime. Thus, a sire's influence may be very widespread as compared to that of a bitch. But in evaluating a particular litter, it must be remembered that the bitch has had as much influence as has had the dog.

Inbreeding, line-breeding, outcrossing, or a combination of the three are the methods commonly used in selective breeding.

Inbreeding is the mating together of closely related animals, such as father-daughter, mother-son, or brother-sister. Although some breeders insist such breeding will lead to the production of defective individuals, it is through rigid inbreeding that all breeds of dogs have been established. Controlled tests have shown that any harmful effects appear within the first five or ten generations, and that if rigid selection is exercised from the beginning, a vigorous inbred strain will be built up.

Line-breeding is also the mating together of individuals related by family lines. However, matings are made not so much on the basis of the dog's and bitch's relationship to each other, but, instead, on the basis of their relationship to a highly admired ancestor, with a view to perpetuating that ancestor's qualities. Line-breeding constitutes a long-range program and cannot be accomplished in a single generation.

Outcrossing is the breeding together of two dogs that are unrelated in family lines. Actually, since breeds have been developed through the mating of close relatives, all dogs within any given breed are related to some extent. There are few breedings that are true outcrosses, but if there is no common ancestor within five generations, a mating is usually considered an outcross.

Experienced breeders sometimes outcross for one generation in order to eliminate a particular fault, then go back to inbreeding or line-breeding. Neither the good effects nor the bad effects of outcrossing can be truly evaluated in a single mating, for undesirable recessive traits may be introduced into a strain, yet not show up for several generations. Outcrossing is better left to experienced breeders, for continual outcrossing results in a wide variation in type and great uncertainty as to the results that may be expected.

Two serious defects that are believed heritable—subluxation and orchidism—should be zealously guarded against, and afflicted dogs and their offspring should be eliminated from breeding programs. Subluxation is a condition of the hip joint where the bone of the socket is eroded and the head of the thigh bone is also worn away, causing lameness which becomes progressively more serious until the dog is unable to walk. Orchidism is the failure of one or both testicles to develop and descend properly. When one testicle is involved, the term "monorchid" is used. When both are involved, "cryptorchid" is used. A cryptorchid is almost always sterile, whereas a monorchid is usually fertile. There is evidence that orchidism "runs in families" and that a monorchid transmits the tendency through bitch and male puppies alike.

Through the years, many misconceptions concerning heredity have been perpetuated. Perhaps the one most widely perpetuated is the idea evolved hundreds of years ago that somehow characteristics were passed on through the mixing of the blood of the parents. We still use terminology evolved from that theory when we speak of bloodlines, or describe individuals as full-blooded, despite the fact that the theory was disproved more than a century ago.

Also inaccurate and misleading is any statement that a definite fraction or proportion of an animal's inherited characteristics can be positively attributed to a particular ancestor. Individuals lacking knowledge of genetics sometimes declare that an individual receives half his inherited characteristics from each parent, a quarter from each grandparent, an eighth from each great-grandparent, etc. Thousands of volumes of scientific findings have been published, but no simple way has been found to determine positively which characteristics have been inherited from which ancestors, for the science of heredity is infinitely complex.

Any breeder interested in starting a serious breeding program should study several of the books on canine genetics and breeding and whelping that are currently available. Two excellent works covering these subjects are *Meisen Breeding Manual,* by Hilda Meisenzahl, and *The Standard Book of Dog Breeding,* by Dr. Alvin Grossman—both published by the publisher of this book.

Whelping box. Detail at right shows proper side-wall construction which helps keep small puppies confined and provides sheltered nook to prevent crushing or smothering.

Breeding and Whelping

The breeding life of a bitch begins when she comes into season the first time at the age of eight to ten months. Thereafter, she will come in season at roughly six-month intervals. Her maximum fertility builds up from puberty to full maturity and then declines until a state of total sterility is reached in old age. Just when this occurs is hard to determine, for the fact that an older bitch shows signs of being in season doesn't necessarily mean she is still capable of reproducing.

The length of the season varies from eighteen to twenty-one days. The first indication is a pronounced swelling of the vulva with coincidental bleeding (called "showing color") for about the first seven to nine days. The discharge gradually turns to a creamy color, and it is during this phase (estrus), from about the tenth to the fifteenth days, that the bitch is ovulating and is receptive to the male. The ripe, unfertilized ova survive for about seventy-two hours. If fertilization doesn't occur, the ova die and are discharged the next time the bitch comes in season. If fertilization does take place, each ovum attaches itself to the walls of the uterus, a membrane forms to seal it off, and a foetus develops from it.

Following the estrus phase, the bitch is still in season until about the twenty-first day and will continue to be attractive to males, although she will usually fight them off as she did the first few days. Nevertheless, to avoid accidental mating, the bitch must be confined for the entire period. Virtual imprisonment is necessary, for male dogs display uncanny abilities in their efforts to reach a bitch in season.

The odor that attracts the males is present in the bitch's urine, so it is advisable to take her a good distance from the house before permitting her to relieve herself. To eliminate problems completely, your veterinarian can prescribe a preparation that will disguise the odor but will not interfere with breeding when the time is right. Many fanciers use such preparations when exhibiting a bitch and find that nearby males show no interest whatsoever. But it is not advisable to permit a bitch to run loose when she has been given a product of this type, for during estrus she will seek the company of male dogs and an accidental mating may occur.

A potential brood bitch, regardless of breed, should have good bone, ample breadth and depth of ribbing, and adequate room in the pelvic region. Unless a bitch is physically mature—well beyond the puppy stage when she has her first season—breeding should be delayed until her second or a later season. Furthermore, even though it is possible for a bitch to conceive twice a year, she should not be bred oftener than once a year. A bitch that is bred too often will age prematurely and her puppies are likely to lack vigor.

Two or three months before a bitch is to be mated, her physical condition should be considered carefully. If she is too thin, provide a rich, balanced diet plus the regular exercise needed to develop strong, supple muscles. Daily exercise on the lead is as necessary for the too-thin bitch as for the too-fat one, although the latter will need more exercise and at a brisker pace, as well as a reduction of food, if she is to be brought to optimum condition. A prospective brood bitch must have had permanent distemper shots as well as rabies vaccination. And a month before her season is due, a veterinarian should examine a stool specimen for worms. If there is evidence of infestation, the bitch should be wormed.

A dog may be used at stud from the time he reaches physical maturity, well on into old age. The first time your bitch is bred, it is well to use a stud that has already proven his ability by having sired other litters. The fact that a neighbor's dog is readily available should not influence your choice, for to produce the best puppies, you must select the stud most suitable from a genetic standpoint.

If the stud you prefer is not going to be available at the time your bitch is to be in season, you may wish to consult your veterinarian concerning medications available for inhibiting the onset of the season. With such preparations, the bitch's season can be delayed indefinitely.

Usually the first service will be successful. However, if it isn't, in most cases an additional service is given free, provided the stud dog is still in the possession of the same owner. If the bitch misses, it may be because her cycle varies widely from normal. Through microscopic examination, a veterinarian can determine exactly when the bitch is entering the estrus phase and thus is likely to conceive.

The owner of the stud should give you a stud-service certificate, providing a four-generation pedigree for the sire and showing the date of mating. The litter registration application is completed only after the puppies are whelped, but it, too, must be signed by the owner of the stud as well as the owner of the bitch. Registration forms may be secured by writing The American Kennel Club.

In normal pregnancy there is visible enlargement of the abdomen by the end of the fifth week. By palpation (feeling with the fingers) a veterinarian may be able to distinguish developing puppies as early as three weeks after mating, but it is unwise for a novice to poke and prod, and try to detect the presence of unborn puppies.

The gestation period normally lasts nine weeks, although it may vary from sixty-one to sixty-five days. If it goes beyond sixty-five days from the date of mating, a veterinarian should be consulted.

During the first four or five weeks, the bitch should be permitted her normal amount of activity. As she becomes heavier, she should be walked on the lead, but strenuous running and jumping should be avoided. Her diet should be well balanced (see page 41), and if she should become constipated, small amounts of mineral oil may be added to her food.

A whelping box should be secured about two weeks before the puppies are due, and the bitch should start then to use it as her bed so she will be accustomed to it by the time puppies arrive. Preferably, the box should be square, with each side long enough so that the bitch can stretch out full length and have several inches to spare at either end. The bottom should be padded with an old cotton rug or other material that is easily laundered. Edges of the padding should be tacked to the floor of the box so the puppies will not get caught in it and smother. Once it is obvious labor is about to begin, the padding should be covered with several layers of spread-out newspapers. Then, as papers become soiled, the top layer can be pulled off, leaving the area clean.

Forty-eight to seventy-two hours before the litter is to be whelped, a definite change in the shape of the abdomen will be noted. Instead of looking barrel-shaped, the abdomen will sag pendulously. Breasts usually redden and become enlarged, and milk may be present a day or two before the puppies are whelped. As the time becomes imminent, the bitch will probably scratch and root at her bedding in an effort to make a nest, and will refuse food and ask to be let out every few minutes. But the surest sign is a drop in temperature of two or three degrees about twelve hours before labor begins.

The bitch's abdomen and flanks will contract sharply when labor actually starts, and for a few minutes she will attempt to expel a puppy, then rest for a while and try again. Someone should stay with the bitch the entire time whelping is taking place, and if she appears to be having unusual difficulties, a veterinarian should be called.

Puppies are usually born head first, though some may be born feet first and no difficulty encountered. Each puppy is enclosed in a separate membranous sac that the bitch will remove with her teeth. She will sever the umbilical cord, which will be attached to the soft, spongy afterbirth that is expelled right after the puppy emerges. Usually the bitch eats the afterbirth, so it is necessary to watch and make sure one is expelled for each puppy whelped. If afterbirth is retained, the bitch may develop peritonitis and die.

The dam will lick and nuzzle each newborn puppy until it is warm and dry and ready to nurse. If puppies arrive so close together that she can't take care of them, you can help her by rubbing the puppies dry with a soft cloth. If several have been whelped but the bitch continues to be in labor, all but one should be removed and placed in a small box lined with clean towels and warmed to about seventy degrees. The bitch will be calmer if one puppy is left with her at all times.

Whelping sometimes continues as long as twenty-four hours for a very large litter, but a litter of two or three puppies may be whelped in an hour. When the bitch settles down, curls around the puppies and nuzzles them to her, it usually indicates that all have been whelped.

The bitch should be taken away for a few minutes while you clean the box and arrange clean padding. If her coat is soiled, sponge it clean before she returns to the puppies. Once she is back in the box, offer her a bowl of warm beef broth and a pan of cool water, placing both where she will not have to get up in order to reach them. As soon as she indicates interest in food, give her a generous bowl of chopped meat to which codliver oil and dicalcium phosphate have been added.

If inadequate amounts of calcium are provided during the period the puppies are nursing, eclampsia may develop. Symptoms are violent trembling, rapid rise in temperature, and rigidity of muscles. Veterinary assistance must be secured immediately, for death may result in a very short time. Treatment consists of massive doses of calcium gluconate administered intravenously, after which symptoms subside in a miraculously short time.

For weak or very small puppies, supplemental feeding is often recommended. Any one of three different methods may be used: tube-feeding (with a catheter attached to a syringe), using an eye-dropper (this method requires great care in order to avoid getting formula in the lungs), or using a tiny bottle (the "pet nurser" available at most pet supply stores). The commercially prepared puppy formulas are most convenient and are readily obtainable from a veterinarian, who can also tell you which method of administering the formula is most practical in your particular case. It is important to remember that equipment must be kept scrupulously clean. It can be sterilized by boiling, or it may be soaked in a Clorox solution, then washed carefully and dried between feedings.

All puppies are born blind and their eyes open when they are ten to fourteen days old. At first the eyes have a bluish cast and appear weak, and the puppies must be protected from strong light until at least ten days after the eyes open.

To ensure proper emotional development, young dogs should be shielded from loud noises and rough handling. Being lifted by the front legs is painful and may result in permanent injury to the shoulders. So when lifting a puppy, always place one hand under the chest with the forefinger between the front legs, and place the other hand under his bottom.

Flannelized rubber sheeting is an ideal surface for the bottom of the bed for the new puppies. It is inexpensive and washable, and will provide a surface that will give the puppies traction so that they will not slip either while nursing or when learning to walk.

Sometimes the puppies' nails are so long and sharp that they scratch the bitch's breasts. Since the nails are soft, they can be trimmed with ordinary scissors.

At about four weeks of age, formula should be provided. The amount fed each day should be increased over a period of two weeks, when the puppies can be weaned completely. One of the commercially prepared formulas can be mixed according to directions on the container, or formula can be prepared at home in accordance with instructions from a veterinarian. The formula should be warmed to lukewarm, and poured into a shallow pan placed on the floor of the box. After his mouth has been dipped into the mixture a few times, a puppy will usually start to lap formula. All puppies should be allowed to eat from the same pan, but be sure the small ones get their share. If they are pushed aside, feed them separately. Permit the puppies to nurse part of the time, but gradually increase the number of meals of formula. By the time the puppies are five weeks old, the dam should be allowed with them only at night. When they are about six weeks old, they should be weaned completely. Three meals a day are usually sufficient from this time until the puppies are about three months old, when feedings are reduced to two a day. About the time the dog reaches one year of age, feedings may be reduced to one each day. (For further information on this subject, see page 38.)

Once they are weaned, puppies should be given temporary distemper injections every two weeks until they are old enough for permanent inoculations. At six weeks, stool specimens should be checked for worms, for almost without exception, puppies become infested. Specimens should be checked again at eight weeks, and as often thereafter as your veterinarian recommends.

Sometimes owners decide as a matter of convenience to have a bitch spayed or a male castrated. While this is recommended when a dog has a serious inheritable defect or when abnormalities of reproductive organs develop, in sound, normal purebred dogs, spaying a bitch or castrating a male may prove a definite disadvantage. The operations automatically bar dogs from competing in shows as well as precluding use for breeding. The operations are seldom dangerous, but they should not be performed without serious consideration of these facts.